Your

Outta Control Ferret

Bobbye Land

T.F.H. Publications, Inc.
One TFH Plaza
Third and Union Avenues
Neptune City, NJ 07753

ISBN: 0-7938-2931-3

Printed and bound in USA .

www.tfh.com

Contents

Knowing more about ferrets and trying to understand them will give you insight into their sometimes unusual behaviors.

This book is meant as a guide to take you through the basics of understanding ferret behavior. Knowing why they do the things they do will hopefully give you insight on how to change the behaviors that are changeable, and learn to deal more easily with, or possibly be able to learn to accept those behaviors that are inherent ferret genetic traits, and therefore, unchangeable. Any ferret has the potential to become unruly and unmanageable very quickly, and with little warning. However, if you take the time to really look at his world, you will usually find something that is amiss in his life that is making him uncomfortable in some way and provoking the unusual behavior. This is something only *you* have the power to change. Be patient. Remember, your ferret buddy is well worth the extra effort to keep him happy and content.

Pet ownership, unlike purchasing a new car or a vacuum cleaner, doesn't come with any real guarantees. Although a responsible breeder may give you a written guarantee that explains how she stands behind the animals she breeds, along with a promise that she can and will offer guidance and support if something goes wrong in the animal's lifetime, there simply is no way that anyone can predict without fail what will happen during the years of a pet's life.

Many a breeder has happily placed a seemingly normal, well-behaved ferret baby with his new family, only to receive a call days, weeks, or

The Name Game

When you're discussing your ferret with a behavior expert or other pet care professional, be sure to use the correct term for your pet's sex. Depending upon the fertile status of the animal, ferrets go by a number of different names:

Kit: baby ferret

Jill: female ferret capable of breeding

Sprite: spayed female

Hob: male ferret capable of breeding

Gib: neutered male

Business: group of ferrets

months later from a panic-stricken owner who insists that her ferret is totally out of control and the breeder's help is needed to correct the situation as soon as possible.

Ferrets require a lot of attention and care. Be sure you know you have the time, patience, and resources to take care of a ferret before you bring one home.

Outta Control Behavior?

It's important to note that the people who see the most "problem ferrets"—those that are handed over to shelters or rescue facilities because they were no longer wanted by their owners—agree that truly serious behavior problems *are not* common in the domestic ferret at all. Only a handful of serious behavior problems are inherent in the animal. Most "problems" are a product of environment and treatment. Very few ferrets actually bite with intent to do damage. A study of reported animal bites was conducted for a full year in New York City (the city that boasts the highest concentration of ferret owners, according to recent surveys of pet ownership). Results revealed over 1000 cat bites, nearly 600 dog bites, over a 100 human bites and *one* (yes, only one) ferret bite. Most vets agree that they would rather see the average pet ferret come into their clinic for treatment than some dog breeds (even though dog breed specific generalizations are as morally and factually incorrect as the general assumption that all ferrets bite and are smelly and unruly).

"Problem ferrets" may just be acting on their instincts. Most "problem behaviors" are the result of environment and treatment.

Although ferrets may "fight" and "wrestle" with each other, they are not aggressive animals.

It's interesting to note that although ferrets have such a bad reputation for being "wicked" and "mean" they are the least likely of any of the pet species to inflict a serious bite. It's also notable that although a rabies vaccination only became approved for ferrets in 1990, there have been fewer than 25 cases of rabid ferrets since 1958, as opposed to the thousands of dogs and cats that tested positive for rabies during that time frame. It's obvious that good public relations for ferrets has been sadly lacking. It's up to you, as a responsible, loving ferret owner to help dispel these ill-founded and untrue rumors by making sure your pet is happy and content, well trained, well cared for, and is a good ambassador for the species.

Defining "Outta Control"

Most people would define an "outta control" ferret as a ferret that no longer happily co-exists with the people and animals he once enjoyed. This is a "monster ferret" that displays exasperating behavior and has

How Did My Ferret Turn Into a Monster?

Think Like a Ferret

If your previously happy-go-lucky ferret suddenly starts exhibiting unacceptable behaviors, put yourself in his place for a while. Think like a ferret and try to see the world through his eyes. Look around you. What is your housing like? Is it neat and clean? Smelly and untidy? Do you get enough to eat? Are you given foods you like to eat? Is your food good for you? Do you get healthy treats and occasional surprises? Is your water supply kept clean? How often are you released from your cage to interact with your human and animal friends? How are you punished when you do something bad? How long has it been since you've visited your doctor for a checkup? Is your cage kept in a busy area of the house so you feel connected to other creatures? Do children or pets in the house make you feel uncomfortable?

Looking at the world through a ferret's perspective may open your eyes to the root of any behavior problems you're experiencing with your ferret.

a multitude of bad habits. Bad behavior reported by a ferret owner could include:

* biting humans and other pets
* refusing to use his litter box
* harassing and fighting with his cage mates
* digging holes in the carpet or being otherwise destructive when given free run of a room or the entire house

Or the ferret might:

* refuse to eat his kibble and dump it outside his cage
* continuously look for a way out of his protected area
* seemingly try to attack his humans when he is turned loose.

A good breeder or seller will be able to point the frantic owner in the right direction to find a solution to these problems, and suggest other ways to avoid potential problems in the future.

Since we've established the fact that very few ferrets are 'born bad," it becomes obvious that a ferret that is suddenly "outta control" is either misunderstood, unhappy, or sick. Any one of these factors is sufficient enough to cause the relationship between a ferret and his owner to deteriorate. The good news is that almost any bad situation can be reversed, and the ferret's natural happy temperament can again surface.

Think about the world from your ferret's point of view. It may give you insight and clues into problem behaviors.

Choosing a Ferret

Choosing the right ferret in the first place is important. People who have spent a lot of time with ferrets (either breeders or pet shop employees) will be able to help you make your choice. Remember, they have been with this animal either for his lifetime (in the case of a breeder) or at least several

Biting is unacceptable for any reason. With time and patience, you can break your ferret out of this bad habit.

Be Responsible

Keep in mind that from the day you bring your ferret home, the proper care for him will be a daily chore. Meeting both his emotional and his physical needs will be an everyday responsibility for you for the rest of his life.

days (in the case of a pet shop employee) and will have had time to notice how he interacts with other ferrets, with strangers, and how he deals with strange situations. Tell the breeder or pet shop employee what kind of lifestyle you have, what you expect from your pet, and then listen to his or her suggestions as to which of the available ferrets might work better in your situation.

Don't be swayed by the color or sex of the ferret. Instead, search for the healthiest, most well adjusted animal you can find. If there is any question about the ferret's health, walk away. A sick ferret is going to be an expensive ferret, and is quite likely to be a ferret that will exhibit

temperament fluctuations as well. Ferrets with chronic health problems will most likely have a lifespan shorter than a healthy ferret. Once you've made the commitment to add a new family member, make sure you choose a ferret that is going to be around as long as possible. Remember that an unhealthy animal is an unhappy animal, and any animal that is not happy will quickly display out of control behavior patterns.

Choose a healthy ferret as your pet. He will be your loving companion for many years.

Alter Your Ferret

Just like humans and other mammals, ferrets go through a period of adolescence when everything is perceived as a potential plaything, a chew toy, or a mate. Spaying or neutering your ferret will help with problems of a sexual nature. If the ferret is descented, it was most likely sterilized at the same time. If neither surgery has been performed, they should be done as soon as possible. This will eliminate a lot of the odors associated with having a ferret in the house, and will also make the ferret a more loving, human-oriented pet, as well as avoid behavior problems associated with puberty and sexual awareness.

Pet behaviorists seem to agree that the first step toward deciding what is truly "out of control" behavior for a pet is to take a long look at not only the species, but also the environment in which the animal

Many patterns of behavior are established when the ferret is young. Knowing what caused the problem is often a key to stopping the unwanted behavior.

How Did My Ferret Turn Into a Monster?

Choose a Healthy Ferret

When choosing your family pet, make certain to pick the healthiest animal you can find. Ferrets are fragile creatures in the best of situations. Bringing home a ferret that is already exhibiting health problems is asking for trouble.

lives and has lived in the past. Knowing the genetic makeup of the species, as well as learning under what conditions it exists now, and where the ferret was bred and raised for his first few weeks of life can usually give behaviorists an idea of what is going, or has already gone wrong. Knowing what caused the problem is a start to knowing how to set things right again. There is almost no problem that cannot be solved with dedication on the part of the pet owner, and a calm, patient attitude.

Remember that a behavior that seems annoying and seemingly unacceptable to you may be completely natural to a ferret. Many times, these typical ferret behaviors have to be dealt with acceptance rather than an attempt at behavior modification. In fact, it may be *your* behavior that needs to be modified, not the ferret's.

Causes of Problems

It may also be necessary to decide whether the problems are "nature versus nurture." In rare circumstances, behavior problems are inherent in certain bloodlines, and thus will be harder to work through than behavior problems caused by human error in training, care, or neglect. Even problems that are genetic in nature are not insurmountable, and with the proper advice from a trainer or behavior modification specialist, and dedication on the part of the pet owner, these "outta control" ferrets can become valued members of the family.

How Can you Tell if a Ferret is Sick?

A sick ferret won't want to be bothered by you or other ferrets. He may show signs of an upper respiratory cold (runny eyes and/or nose), and you might hear him sneeze. A ferret that has been sick for a while will be thin and his hair will look dull and lifeless. He'll be listless and lethargic and even though he may tug at your heart-strings, you will have to be realistic, and keep looking for the right ferret...a healthy ferret.

Health Issues

Behavior problems can also be a symptom of health issues. The first place you should go with your new ferret, even before you take the ferret home, is to your veterinarian for a complete checkup. Make certain that you've done your homework in choosing your vet, and found someone who has many other happy, healthy ferret clients. She will know what to look for to assure you that the ferret you've chosen should be around for a long time.

Even though you may have started out with a healthy pet, behavior problems can indicate possible health concerns. None of us stay healthy all the time. There will always be disease, illness, and injuries to wreak havoc in our lives. It's the same

A sick ferret will generally appear listless and may sleep more than usual. Take your ferret to the vet if you suspect he is ill.

How Did My Ferret Turn Into a Monster?

An annual veterinary checkup will ensure that your ferret stays healthy and happy.

with our pets. Ask your vet what symptoms you should be on the lookout for. Always take your ferret to the vet when you've noticed any abnormal behavior in your pet. What you perceive as "monster" behavior may instead be a symptom of an illness.

An adrenal problem in ferrets is one health issue (very serious and possibly life-threatening) that can cause a normally well-behaved member of the family to turn into an unmanageable pest. Caught early, even the more serious health issues can have a good prognosis, and hopefully your pet will soon resume his normal, loving behavior patterns. Even non-serious health problems, such as teething in a young ferret, or a bump or bruise on an older one, can cause a normally sweet and outgoing ferret to withdraw and become grumpy. Think about how you feel when you have a headache. You'd probably want to bite the hand that plucked you out of your warm, cozy bed and demanded that you entertain him.

Unlike most other pets, the ferret is susceptible to all human disorders, including communicable diseases. Unfortunately, there are few medicines and antibiotics that are truly effective once a ferret gets really sick. (However, baby strength Amoxicillin seems to work for simple colds or relatively minor infections.) For that reason, it's very important to stay away from your ferret while you're ill. The chances are too high that he will become sick and might not be able to recover.

Adjusting to Adoption

A ferret that has been abused or neglected in a previous situation is

Creature Comforts

Although ferrets appear to be closely related to wild animals, they are completely domesticated to the point where they rely on their owners for every aspect of their life, including the need to socialize. Your ferret will never be happy left alone all day in a cage, even in an enormous cage filled with toys and treats. A ferret is very much like a young child. If you can imagine the scenario presented if a young child was locked in a room alone, with nothing but a plate of food, some water, and a few toys, then you can imagine why a ferret does the things he does when he's bored and lonely. Old or young, ferrets need at the minimum a couple of hours per day to run loose in a closely supervised and protected area of your home. They want to be in close proximity with their family of humans and animal friends.

Pretty much all a ferret will ask for from life is to be allowed to run and play, to have toys that stretch his imagination, to bond with animal or human friends, to eat food he finds tasty, and to have plenty of time for nice long uninterrupted naps in a snuggly hammock in a clean cage. Provide him with these simple pleasures, and you may find that many of the "problem behaviors" you are currently experiencing will disappear.

How Did My Ferret Turn Into a Monster?

going to take a period of adjustment and training before he can be trusted...and before he will trust you. Where there is no trust, you can't be sure that the behavior patterns you're seeing are the ferret's true nature. He may be exhibiting behaviors he doesn't really feel, and throwing up a smoke screen to make you back off.

Gaining his trust should be the first step before you attempt to modify any behaviors in a "second-hand" ferret. It's always possible that once the ferret becomes comfortable in his new situation, whatever the previous owner did to inspire the problem behavior may disappear when that prior stimulus is removed. Give the ferret a chance to show you his true personality before you begin any retraining or behavior modification practices.

Ferrets are naturally curious animals and will explore everything in your household. Set limits so your ferret knows what is and isn't acceptable.

Some behaviors are just peculiar to individual animals. After all, all humans don't have the same temperament or behave the same way in the same situations. Why should we expect anything different from our animal companions? Don't try so hard to make the perfect pet out of your ferret that you completely smother his individual character.

You should always give any new addition to the family some careful scrutiny to be certain that what you're seeing is truly a "bad behavior" and is not a misunderstanding on your part. It is always possible that his "bad behavior" was considered acceptable or even amusing and precocious in a previous home, yet might be something you will want to change as soon as possible. An adjustment period may be necessary before a firm schedule can be adapted for housetraining, behavior modification, etc. if your pet is new to your household, no matter what his age.

Another oft-forgotten point to consider if you adopt a previously owned ferret is whether or not he lived in a home with smokers. Many animal behaviorists firmly believe that a pet that has lived with heavy smokers will go through nicotine withdrawal and that the animal reacts to this about like a human being would in that situation. If you've ever been around someone who's trying to stop smoking, you can imagine how disturbing, frustrating (and normal-behavior altering) this can be for a ferret who doesn't really understand why he feels the way he does. Ask any heavy smoker who is going through withdrawal, and he'll tell you that he feels like biting or snapping at someone most of the time.

Keep a Routine

Ferrets are creatures of routine. They will go to the bathroom where their litter box has been, even if the box is removed. Therefore, they will not do well with a family who constantly experiences life-altering changes such as moving. Ferrets enjoy a routine as long as it is fulfilling

Non-Problem Behaviors

If you have purchased a well-bred, healthy animal that has previously lived in a good situation with knowledgeable and caring ferret owners, more often than not, the "unacceptable behavior" that the pet is exhibiting may be nothing more than retaliation for (real or imagined) slights, incorrect training, housing, or other treatment on the part of the previous owner. Quite simply, these are not problems at all, but are a breach of communication between pet and owner.

In the case of ferrets, sometimes the problems arise because the owner hasn't researched the species enough to realize that what they perceive as "abnormal" and "outta control" is simply a totally normal ferret, exhibiting totally normal ferret behavior. A ferret's actions that seem scary and unpredictable to an uneducated owner will be the very actions that a seasoned ferret owner will consider cute and endearing. The beauty of ferrets oftentimes truly does lie in the eye of the beholder.

and contains enough variety (such as occasional new toys and bedding) to keep them entertained. If your family is constantly on the move, or has a pattern of not following routines in other areas, make sure that the part of the world that actually touches your ferret changes as little as possible. If you do move, make certain that the same furniture and rugs are in the room that the ferret has access to. Set up his cage in exactly the same way, in as nearly the same location as in the previous house (facing a window, or near a door, or under a light fixture, where he can see the TV, or some other basic fixture that will be much the same in any house). Record the old radio station from home so your ferret can hear it in the new house. Or play the same channels on TV. Keep as much routine as possible and you'll have fewer problems with the way your ferret adjusts to the new situation.

Ferret Communication

Ferrets are currently the third most popular pets in the US (following closely behind dogs and cats). There are an estimated eight to ten million ferrets in the US being kept as pets, even in states and cities where they are considered illegal. Unfortunately, many of these pets were chosen without thought to the long-term ramifications of choosing not only a pet, but a ferret, who comes with a whole long list of unique needs and responsibilities.

Most of the ferrets in animal shelters and with ferret rescue groups didn't end up there because their behavior problems were insurmountable—more often than not they were abandoned because their owners weren't willing to take the time to get to know the ferrets, and try to understand what they were attempting to tell them through the only means of communication available, sounds and actions. How much easier would it be to live with and train a ferret if they could talk? Since they can't, it's up to the dedicated owner to try to learn the ferret's language.

As you get to know your ferret better, you will learn that his body language alone can tell you quite a bit about what he is feeling and what he wants. What can be perceived as aggressive behavior to someone who doesn't understand "Ferret-ese" will be understood

Your ferret may be trying to communicate with you through body language and noises. Observe your ferret and take the time to learn his different moods.

How Did My Ferret Turn Into a Monster?

Strange Behavior

If your ferret dances (flings himself about on all fours with an arched back), clucks, races around careening into walls (or furniture, or people), bares his teeth, waggles his tail, or puffs his tail "bottle-brush" style, he hasn't really gone insane and he likely isn't angry with you—he's just being a ferret and engaging in some totally normal ferret hi-jinks.

by someone who reads ferret body talk as simply a barometer of the ferret's mood and not an indication of a bad temperament or behavior problem.

Ferrets do not try to avoid running into things (probably because their vision is poor and because they are usually moving at high speed). Many new owners have called their veterinarians in a panic, fearing that the ferret is having convulsions, has rabies, or has gone blind. I'm sure most vets have to hide a smile as they reassure the excited owner that what they are describing is normal ferret behavior and nothing to be concerned about. This is simply the ferret's way of expressing his exuberance at being let out to play, and instead of a symptom of ill health, it is a very good indicator that the ferret is feeling normal. Ferrets seem to have a very high threshold of pain and do not appear to notice bumps and knocks that would make most other animals stop and lick the spot that got hurt.

If your ferret jumps out at you from beneath the dust ruffle of your couch and grabs your ankles, he's playing, and not really attacking you. If he nips during that play, he's simply forgotten that you're not as tough as another ferret, and he needs a gentle reminder that you're a tender-skinned human. If he chases you as you walk around the room, he's not intent on doing bodily damage to you, but attempting to start a game of tag. Want him to settle down? Stop moving and he'll quickly find another target of interest.

Your Outta Control Ferret

Body Language of the Ferret

Almost every movement that a ferret makes means something. It's definitely worth your while to spend some time learning ferret language—their body language at least!

Hopping, Jumping, and Bouncing Toward you

People sometimes think this means that the ferret is 'after them.' Indeed, sometimes it does look like he's lunging towards you in an aggressive action, but this is actually a ploy on the part of the ferret to engage you in play. Think of a baby kitten making the same moves, and you can easily see what's going on in your ferret's mind. Making a jump towards him at this point will instigate a gleeful game of chase and tag for your ferret. If you're not in the mood for a game, simply sit or stand still, he'll find a more interesting target.

A ferret's body language is the best indicator of his mood and what he is thinking. Pay close attention to your pet and try to understand what he is trying to tell you.

Back Arched, Clucking

This is another game gesture. Again, think of a baby kitten arching its back, meowing loudly, as it sidesteps toward a littermate in a mock battle. Your ferret is simply talking to you, and inviting you (or his cage mate) to join in some speedy ferret games. Getting down on his level and using your hand as a combatant for him (arching your hand with your fingers on the floor, spider like, and walking your fingers toward him, and away from him) will likely send him into paroxysms of delight.

Running Backward

This will happen sometimes as you try to pick up your ferret. Although this may appear to be a fear gesture (and in the case of a ferret you don't know well, assume that it's a likely indication that he was abused in a prior home and take special measures to gain his trust), it is most likely the same action a toddler might make when he's told it's time to stop playing and take a nap. Your ferret is not ready to go to bed (his cage) just yet, so he backs away from you, hoping to squeeze in a few extra moments of playtime (chasing him at this point would be sheer delight for him.)

To break this habit, pick up your ferret often while he is outside his cage for playtime, give him a tasty treat, a quick caress, and then put him back down for more play. This way he does not always associate being picked up with being immediately put away.

Puffing

When your ferret sits up tall, on all four feet, with his back slightly arched and all the hair on his body and tail standing on end, it's very likely that something has either startled him, or he is the loser in a spat between himself and a battle partner. A ferret does this to make himself appear larger, and thus more formidable than he really is. This is also considered a fear gesture and is often seen in ferrets that have been abused.

Putting Teeth on your Hand While he's Being Held

Unless this is done in a nip action, putting his teeth on your hand is a ferret's way of asking (in his way of thinking, at least) to be put down. He could also be warning you to not hurt him. Never jerk your hand away at this time, but instead use a training word such as "No," or "Careful," or "Stop!" as a warning that this action is unacceptable.

Continue holding the ferret for a few more minutes. Giving in to him and putting him down is a bad idea, as you'll be letting him know that the action scared you. This will create a problem as he learns to use his teeth to get his way. Be firm, but gentle in not giving into this action. Remember that you are dealing with a ferret here, not a Rottweiler. While a ferret's bite is certainly not fun, and it can draw blood, it won't do any lasting damage, and letting your pet have the last word (or tooth) in the matter can have a long-term detrimental effect to your relationship.

Sound Language

Not only do ferrets have an extensive body language repertoire, but their sound language is fairly extensive too. Don't worry if your ferret doesn't make much noise. Most of them don't, most of the time. You'll quickly learn what they're feeling by the sounds they make, as well as their actions.

Clucking

This sound can range from a cluck or chuckle to what owners call a "dook dook" noise. Until you know your ferret well, or unless you have an excellent understanding of other ferret body language, it's sometimes hard to tell whether the ferret is very happy, or very angry. Usually however, this indicates happiness or excitement and is often uttered while playing or exploring a new area. This seems to be an 'all-purpose' noise,

Noise

Most ferrets don't make much noise. This doesn't necessarily mean they're unhappy, just that you're lucky enough to have chosen a quiet one. Like people, some ferrets are more vocal than others. While one ferret may race dizzily around the room clucking and dooking at the top of his voice in an excited frenzy, his cagemate may be racing around equally dizzily, but without making a sound. Both are exhibiting behavior that is normal for them as individuals, as well as members of the ferret family.

and ferrets use it frequently to express a variety of emotions. It appears to most people that when the noise is associated with anger or fear, the noise seems to be a little more high-pitched and more rapid.

Whimpering/Whining

Young ferrets (kits) especially, do this as a general excitement noise. It can also be uttered by the loser in a wrestling match.

Hissing

This is more the sound of fear than aggression, although sometimes a ferret that is growing weary of unwanted attention from another ferret will use a hiss as a warning to back off.

Screaming, Screeching, or Very High-Pitched "Chittering"

This indicates extreme fright or pain. This is your cue that it's time to go rescue your pet from whatever he's gotten himself into. It can also be a sign of extreme anger. A ferret that truly screams is in pain.

Living with a Ferret

Since you've purchased this book, it's obvious you're a dedicated pet owner, trying to figure out how to handle a behavior problem of some sort with your ferret. Or perhaps you're an exceptionally savvy pet owner who wants to know what to do about a problem before it occurs. An ounce of prevention truly is worth a pound of cure, as the old saying goes.

Now that we've gone through the positive aspects of suspected behavior problems, hopefully you'll never have serious behavior problems with your ferret, but that's not to say they aren't possible! Anyone who's spent time with ferrets will tell you that this is not a typical cat or a dog or a rodent. Ferrets are *not* for everyone. Although the species is domesticated, ferrets are, by nature of their genetics, cunning and sly. Their ancestors were bred to be hunters, and that "searching for prey" instinct is still very much a part of their makeup. Ferrets are members of the Mustelidae family, which includes weasels, otters, polecats, badgers, and minks. Many ferret owners refer lovingly to their ferrets as "weasels," the animal they most closely resemble.

Ferrets are unique pets and are not suited for everyone. They are guided by their instincts and love to explore their surroundings.

How Did My Ferret Turn Into a Monster?

Ferrets were first domesticated around 2000 to 3000 years ago and they were used as hunting animals for centuries before assuming a role as a household pet. Although settlers did bring some ferrets to America, ferret populations in the US were never high until they were imported by the government as a method of controlling rodent populations in granaries in the 1800s. When some of these ferrets decided that fresh chicken was better for supper than rodents, poultry farmers raised a hue and cry to have limits put on the ferret population and discontinue their use as a rodent deterrent. Due to the resulting government regulations and vigilant care in monitoring breeders, there are no wild ferret colonies in this country. Although domesticated ferrets would have a slim chance of making it in the wild, the chance that a particularly savvy pair could establish a colony was behind the reasoning of the laws passed in almost every state making it illegal to turn a ferret loose. Not only is such an action inhumane, but also it can cost you money (or jail time) if you're caught.

As frustrating as some ferret behavior problems are that plague owners today, these are the very traits that early owners found most attractive for their purposes:

* Biting: Necessary for killing prey (rodents).
* Digging: Necessary to search and destroy prey.
* Ability to 'ferret" his way into almost any tight space: Necessary for hunting rats.
* Being cunning and sly: Necessary to be a formidable adversary for savvy prey.
* Housetraining: The fact that ferrets are not necessarily creatures of habit with their toilet practices put their scent over a wider area, which was a deterrent for rodent populations in granaries.

Although it is the nature of a ferret to be sweet, loving and charming, sometimes those characteristics are overshadowed by those less desirable traits harkening back to their early roots. In that case, you must learn to handle each situation in the correct manner to create a bond of trust between the two of you. With just a little time and effort, you can turn even an 'outta control' ferret into a charming and endearing member of the family.

Proper
Care for
Fewer Problems

In This Chapter You'll Learn:

✱ Proper medical care

✱ How to recognize symptoms of illness

✱ How to provide for your ferret's basic needs

✱ How to train your ferret properly, using correct
methods

Working through any problems that arise with your ferret will be a major waste of time unless you continue doing "relationship maintenance" throughout your pet's life. Just as it is true with humans that "you have to be a friend to have a friend," it is equally true with your ferret. Continue with the positive reinforcements, the quality play times, the treats, and the gentle corrections. Provide adequate housing and feeding and daily care as well as the other normal maintenance, and you and your ferret can truly be friends for what will hopefully be a long, healthy, and productive life.

A veterinarian will give your ferret a complete physical exam on his first visit and make sure that he is in good health.

Health Care

Being your ferret's best friend will not only warm the cockles of your heart and enrich your life, but will also mean that you will be more in tune to his emotions, physical actions, and reactions than will someone

Finding a Veterinarian

The American Veterinary Medical Association (AVMA) can assist you in locating a veterinarian near you that specializes in "exotics" (which will hopefully include ferrets).

American Veterinary Medical Association
1931 North Meacham Road - Suite 100
Schaumburg, IL 60173
Phone: (847) 925-8070
Fax: (847) 925-1329
Email: avmainfo@avma.org

who merely exists in the same home with their pet. You will find it doesn't take a pet psychic to tell when something is bothering your furry friend once you have familiarized yourself with his routines, his play behavior, and his daily routines. Something that might have gone unnoticed to a less caring pet owner will send you racing to the vet at the first hint of a possible health problem that might have gone on without treatment for days, weeks, or even longer, had you not noticed a minor variation in your ferret's normal routine.

It's a good idea to find a veterinarian who is experienced in ferret health care before a medical emergency arises. Find a vet who treats "exotics" in your area.

It's a very good idea to visit the veterinarian's office before you take your ferret in for a checkup. Prepare a few questions to ask before you make the final decision that this is the vet you want to have working on your ferret. Some important questions to ask include:

1. How many ferret clients do you see? How often?
2. Do you have ferrets of your own?
3. What are your emergency call guidelines?
4. Will you come to the office after hours in case of an emergency? Where will you refer me if you could not?
5. Have you done continuing education regarding ferrets? Do you keep up to date with ferret-specific medicine?

* Something only slightly abnormal can alert you to possibly severe problems. For instance, one of the early symptoms of adrenal problems is an aggressive tendency being displayed in a heretofore placid animal. Adrenal problems will occur in almost half of our domestic ferrets during their lifetimes, and although it can be treated, the faster it is diagnosed, the less costly it will be for you and less life-threatening it will be for your pet.

* Insulinoma also creates some behavior problems as early symptoms. Your vet may call it by a different name such as pancreatic tumors, hypoglycemia, or "low" blood sugar. But by any name, the list of symptoms will almost always include one or more of the following odd behaviors: staring into space, staggering, drooling, fainting spells, clenched teeth or locked jaws, moaning or crying aloud, or, in an advanced seizure, screaming.

* Ferrets can get hairballs, just like cats do, but because of the way their digestive system is designed, ferrets do not vomit up hairballs. Instead, the hairballs remain in the stomach, causing lack of appetite with eventual weight loss, irritability and debilitation, and requiring extensive (and possibly life-threatening) surgery to correct. Administering a feline hairball remedy a few times each week will help prevent this.

Scratching

Ferrets are itchy little creatures, and a certain amount of scratching seems to be normal for most. Even seeing them wake up from a deep sleep for what appears to be a scratching emergency is normal. However, itching can also be a sign of several problems.

Of course, the most common malady that can cause a ferret to itch is that he has picked up fleas that have been brought indoors by the dog or cat. If you look closely at his belly, you'll see either the fleas scurrying for safety, or bits of "flea dirt" that look like black specks of pepper. This is actually bits of dried blood left behind after the fleas have bitten your pet.

To get rid of the fleas, you can use almost any product that says it is "safe for use on kittens." Products containing pyrethrins are okay, but don't use anything that contains organophosphates, carbamates or petroleum distillates. Follow all directions carefully and consult your vet if you have questions on flea products for ferrets.

Be sure to treat the ferret's cage and bedding, too. You can use a premise spray directly around the cage, but you'll likely find you'll have to bomb the entire house as well. Get a flea bomb that contains methoprene (a flea growth regulator) that will interrupt the growth cycles. Of course you should remove the ferrets from the house while you're flea bombing. Before you bomb, also make sure you wash all of the ferret's bedding (in hot water) and vacuum the house.

Ferrets are generally clean animals. If you notice your ferret scratching a lot, he may have fleas. Consult your veterinarian for the proper treatment.

Proper Care for Fewer Problems

Other possible reasons for excessive itching if no fleas are present include: dry skin, food allergies (or allergic reactions to cleaning supplies or laundry detergents), bacterial or fungal infections, mites, or a nutrition imbalance caused by feeding an improper diet. Excessive itching and hair loss are symptoms of adrenal failure, so be sure to see a vet if you're concerned. Even if the itching isn't caused by something serious, the scratching can create an infection that may require veterinary attention.

If your neutered male suddenly tries to mate his ferret friends (or the family cat, or another small animal), dribbles urine, or marks his areas excessively, becomes overly aggressive, or has penile erections, it could likely be because of an unusual hormone production that is probably caused by adrenal disease. Other possibilities include cryptorchidism (a testicle that never descended into the scrotum and wasn't removed during neutering. Therefore he is technically "un-neutered" and is simply displaying normal fertile ferret hormonal behavior patterns.) or he could have bladder stones. The treatment for any of these conditions is surgery.

Keep an Eye on Your Ferret

Because ferrets are small and have fast metabolisms, they can become seriously ill very quickly. The good news is that because you're a responsible pet owner, you'll notice the symptoms quickly, and get your ferret the proper health care. A ferret that receives prompt medical attention is capable of recuperating almost as quickly as he got sick.

A ferret can become ill quickly. If you notice that something seems "off" with your pet, or if he refuses to eat and appears lifeless, take him to the vet. Don't try to diagnose illnesses on your own.

It's a very good idea to keep a record of the normal temperature, heart rate, and respiration rate for your individual ferrets. That way you will have a baseline number to quote when telling your veterinarian why you suspect a medical problem. Most ferrets will have a rectal temperature of 100-103° F, with 101.9° being the average. Ferrets generally have a heart rate of 216-250 beats per minute (with 225 being the average), and a normal respiration of 33-36 breaths per minute.

The commitment to continue the very best possible veterinary health care is only part of the commitment to being your ferret's best friend. Besides the care that your veterinarian will provide (rabies and distemper vaccinations, fecal checks, and dewormings if necessary, as well as a complete physical at least once a year) you will be responsible for your pet's daily and weekly maintenance health care for the rest of his life.

Proper Care for Fewer Problems

Medication

You should never give your ferret any medication that has not been prescribed by your veterinarian. Medication that can cure problems in humans or other species can be fatal to ferrets. Not only will dosages differ from species to species, but some human medications are extremely toxic to ferrets.

As with a ferret who suddenly turns up his nose at his food dish, anytime a normally very active ferret sleeps more than usual, or doesn't seem interested in playing with you or other ferrets at all, a trip to the vet is in order. It's better to be safe than sorry, and if an otherwise routine visit alerts your vet to an imminent problem, you will have a far lower bottom line on the final bill than with an emergency call later on. Once your vet realizes how carefully tuned in to your pet you are, he will begin trusting your opinions more and more, and you can become true partners in your pet's health welfare treatments and decisions.

Feeding

Proper health maintenance includes feeding a food that is specially formulated for ferrets. For many years, the common recommendation from breeders and veterinarians was to feed a ferret a good quality dry cat or kitten food. While ferrets, on a basic level do have similar dietary requirements to cats, their intestines are built differently. Food passes through a ferret's digestive system rapidly and they have the ability to process vegetable matter. A ferret's diet must be very high in animal protein, relatively high in fat, and very low in fiber.

Choosing a food that does not meet all your ferret's nutritional needs can be the first step on the road to behavior problems that can be caused from dietary and nutritional imbalances. Even dry foods that

38

Feed your ferret food especially designed for ferrets. They should not be fed cat or dog food.

are formulated especially for ferrets are not alike, so do your homework before you decide what your ferret will be eating.

The food should have 30-35% protein and 15-20% fat. Animal protein (preferably chicken) should be the first Ingredient and at least two or three of the next few ingredients. Be sure you read the ingredient label, and not just the name of the foods with ferret pictures on the bags. Most of them weren't designed for ferrets; they were originally formulated for minks or cats and maybe modified slightly, and then marketed at a higher price for ferrets.

Food formulated expressly for ferrets will be more expensive than cat or mink food, but your ferret will actually eat less and, as an added bonus, will defecate less too! Mink and cat foods have more fish oil than ferrets really need, and the fish oil definitely adds to the bad smell in the litter pan.

Proper Care for Fewer Problems

If you have more than one ferret, consider giving each ferret his own food dish to prevent squabbling at dinnertime.

Ferrets enjoy healthy snacks and treats, such as crackers, dry cereal, and raisins.

Treats

Suggestions for treats include: peanut butter on a bit of cracker, mashed banana, raisins, nuts, freeze-dried liver (sold as cat treats), and puffed rice cakes. You can feed your ferret anything that can be broken into small pieces. You never know what is going to be considered a special treat to him. If you find a treat that is good for him, as well as tasty, be sure to keep some on hand in case your ferret gets sick and needs special tempting to get him to eat.

Although your ferret might enjoy fresh fruits and vegetables as treats, you should be sure that they do not eat enough of them to ruin their appetite for their kibble. They cannot digest plant matter, so all they will get from a fruit or veggie treat is the taste, and no nutritional value.

Your ferret should have a balanced diet and access to his food at all times. Be sure the food you feed your pet is fresh. Your ferret will appreciate it.

"Duck Soup"

For a ferret that is recuperating from an illness, or an elderly ferret that needs special nutrition, most breeders and veterinarians suggest feeding a home-made "soup" that most refer to as "Duck Soup."

"Duck Soup"

1 can *Sustacal, Ensure, or other human nutrition supplement (8 oz)

1 can water (8 oz)

2 scoops puppy or kitten weaning formula — OPTIONAL

4 oz. dry kitten or ferret food, soaked in enough water to cover and soften it completely

(*You can substitute ready-to-eat milk-replacement for kittens)

Mix thoroughly. Feed at room temperature, about 4 fluid ounces at a time, twice a day for maintenance. If your ferret begins to gain too much weight too quickly, dilute the mixture with a bit of water. This formula freezes well, so it's always a good idea to have a couple of days supply in the freezer in case of emergency.

Fat Ferrets

Obesity is a common problem in ferrets. It can lead to many serious health issues and can even be fatal if allowed to continue unchecked. Lack of proper exercise is the leading cause of obesity in ferrets, although some ferrets are more prone to overeat than others.

Whatever you decide to feed, make sure that the ferret's bowl is always full of fresh kibble. Make sure that the kibble isn't moldy or attracting moths or flies, and that clean, cool water is available nearby. Most ferrets will appreciate having not only a drip bottle for their water, but also a bowl for lapping (and for dipping their toes into on warm days).

What you feed your ferret, how much, and how often will determine his weight. Just like humans, ferrets come in all different sizes and body shapes. A healthy adult male can be anywhere from 2 to 5 pounds, and a female about half that. Ferrets, especially males, normally gain more weight in the winter and then lose it again in the spring. Some ferrets have a stockier built than others, which can make one appear heavier than another longer and leaner ferret. When you run your hand down your ferret's side, you should feel his muscles ripple a

An occasional ferret treat is fine, but make sure your pet doesn't become spoiled on them. Overfeeding can lead to obesity and other health problems.

bit and be able to feel the ribs, but they shouldn't stick out or feel too bony. Little "love handles" are common in the winter. If your pet feels

Poisoned Foods?

We know that pesticides and other chemicals that are used in growing fruits and vegetables for human consumption are not good for us. Consider how dangerous they can potentially be for our ferrets that have digestive systems far more sensitive and smaller than our own. Some chemicals can cause hormone imbalances that can create or worsen existing behavioral problems. Buy organically grown foods whenever possible!

Proper Care for Fewer Problems

soft and "mushy" or looks pear-shaped, he might be overweight, or just have poor muscle tone from insufficient exercise. Try letting him exercise more often, for longer periods of time, and try cut back a bit on his food.

Home Life

Ferret-Proofing

Before your ferret is allowed free run of any area outside his cage, canvass it thoroughly and check for small objects that may have been dropped on the floor, cigarette butts in ashtrays (many a curious ferret has died from nicotine poisoning after stealing and eating cigarette butts), buckets of mop water (curiosity kills ferrets much more often than it kills cats), teetering piles of books or magazines or boxes that could easily crush the ferret who careens blindly into them at a dead run, or any of a hundred other possible dangers. Creating a safe haven

Be sure to ferret-proof your home before you let your ferret out of his cage. Medications, electrical cords, and other hazards should be kept out of your ferret's reach.

44

for your ferret isn't something that can be done once and then forgotten. Be aware every time your pet is turned loose and avoid tragedy.

Toys

When you're choosing ferret toys, make sure they can withstand rough treatment. Check to see that they don't have small parts that can be chewed off and swallowed (such as bells or bows). Your ferret will appreciate a change of toys from time to time. Instead of giving him every toy he owns all at

Household Dangers

Ferrets can get into almost anything. Be sure to keep a close eye on your pet and keep small objects away from him. Beware of the following choking hazards:

Rubber bands, pen tops, ribbons, bows, paper clips, bottle caps, and anything that can be broken or chewed into pieces smaller than a ping pong ball.

Ferrets are inquisitive creatures and will help themselves to anything they find interesting. Keep an eye on your pet to make sure he doesn't swallow small objects he finds around the house.

Keep your ferret busy by giving him interesting toys to play with. They like to crawl through plastic hosing and create tunnels to explore.

one time, give him only a few, and exchange them occasionally. He'll react to old favorites as if seeing them for the very first time. If his behavior problems stem from boredom, keeping a ferret entertained with lots of new playthings may be an immediate fix to the situation.

Cleanliness

Keeping your ferret and his surroundings clean will help inhibit health problems that are prone to arise in unclean situations. You'll find that a lot of the odor associated with ferrets comes not from the ferrets themselves, or even from their litter pan, but, instead from their bedding which absorbs quite a lot of their musky body odor very quickly. Be sure you choose bedding that is easily washable, and wash it very often. Adding a few drops of bleach to the wash cycle and fabric softener to the rinse water will help get rid of any lingering odor. Have extra snuggle sacks and hammocks so that your ferret won't be

46

Your ferret will be happy and well-adjusted if you keep his surroundings safe and clean.

uncomfortable during wash times (some ferret hammocks and snuggle sacks should not be dried in the drier, so they'll need to be out of the cage until they're thoroughly line dried.) In a pinch, you can always toss

Security Gates

Finding a gate that will keep your ferret in a particular room or portion of the house is challenging, but once you've found one that works for you, you'll realize it's worth its weight in gold. Only a very closely supervised ferret should be allowed to roam freely through the house. Even the most well-behaved and best-trained ferret can quickly get into trouble when allowed too much freedom. Keep one area of your home accessible to him when he's out of his cage, and keep the off limits areas either behind closed doors, or behind adequate gating.

an old pair of shorts or t-shirt into their cage to be used as a sleeping bag while their usual bedding is being cleaned.

Home Sweet Home

Your ferret's cage should be a safe haven where he knows he is protected and can sleep without fear of being rudely interrupted. Allowing his cage to become like a prison by keeping him in involuntary lockdown all day long is one of the starting points for behavior problems.

Your ferret's cage is his happy little home. Make sure that the cage is sturdy and large enough to house the ferret, his toys, bedding, litter pan, and food dishes. The bigger the cage, the better!

Because your ferret will be in his cage for so much of the time, even allowing for the few hours a day he is allowed free access to a room or your entire house, you should make sure that you choose a cage that is as large as your budget and space will allow. A good size for a home cage is 2 x 3 feet and 2 feet high (60 x 100 x 60 cm). For traveling, or for vet trips a carry cage 1 x 2 x 1 feet (30 x 60 x 30 cm) should be sufficient.

Multi-level cages make great homes for ferrets. They not only get exercise racing from top to bottom, and leaping from level to level, but they can choose

different sleeping areas throughout the day, providing a change of
scenery not available in a single or
double-level cage. Having trays at
different levels will also allow
space for hanging hammocks and
snuggle sacks that your ferret will
enjoy.

Any cage should have more than
one opening, and in the case of a
cage that is several feet tall, the

Cage Size

A ferret that is kept in
a too-small cage will likely
become neurotic and will
not be easily tamed or
trained. Proper housing is
just as important to a
ferret as any other
aspect of routine pet
care…in fact more impor-
tant than some.

openings should be adjacent to each level, to allow you easy access to
toys, food dishes, and bedding.

Place the ferret's cage in a busy part of the household so he has
plenty of interesting diversions to attract his attention.

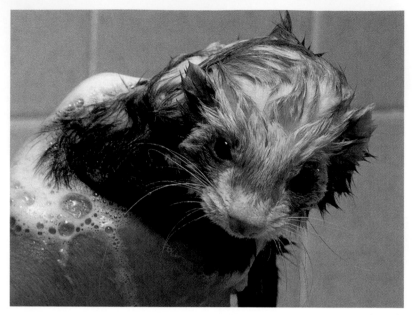

Unless your ferret has gotten into something sticky or messy, he generally will not need a bath. Excess bathing can dry out his skin.

Bathing

Although some people bathe their ferrets regularly, it seems to be a popular consensus that unless your ferret gets into something unpleasant or sticky, or has a bad case of fleas, you really don't need to bathe him very often. Bathing doesn't affect the odor much, in fact, many people say that ferrets smell *worse* for a few days following a bath. The best thing you can do to control your ferret's scent is to change his bedding every few days and keep the litter pans clean (by either totally changing the litter every few days, or scooping it out daily). Most ferret breeders agree that giving an annual bath is acceptable. They say that bathing once a month is okay too, but bathing your ferret more frequently can cause problems with dry skin, especially in winter months.

Most ferrets don't seem to mind baths. In fact, some ferrets actually seem to enjoy their bath time quite a bit, and swim around in the tub and dive for the drain plug. Giving them floating toys to bat about can make bath time an even more positive experience for them, and it is excellent exercise for a bored ferret.

How to Bathe Your Ferret

Fill a tub or kitchen sink partway with warm water. Many people have found that ferrets prefer their baths warmer than they expect, probably because a ferret's body temperature is pretty high. You don't want to scald your ferret, but if you can put your hand into the water and feel comfortable right away, it should be okay. If your ferret is one that enjoys water, you may want to give him time to play in the water. Fill the basin just deeper than the ferret is tall, and provide some sort of support (a floating ring, or a box turned upside down In the water) in case he gets tired of swimming. You might also want to consider taking him into the shower with you. Many ferrets that don't like baths are perfectly happy being held in a shower.

Once playtime is over, it's time to get serious about the cleaning portion (remember, that's the reason you're here in the first place) of the bath. Use a shampoo that is suitable for young cats and kittens. Always ask your veterinarian before using a shampoo that contains any kind of harsh chemical (such as flea or other insect control, etc.). Specially formulated ferret shampoos are

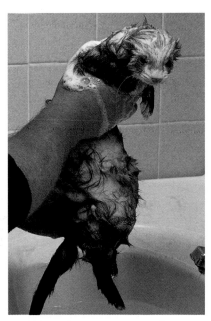

Keep a firm grip on your ferret while bathing him. Talk to him in a soothing voice if he becomes nervous or afraid.

available, and many owners agree that human no-tears baby shampoo works fine too.

Wet the ferret completely, and lather him from head to tail. Most ferrets will start to struggle at this point. Letting them put their hind legs on a towel draped over the side of the tub while they're being washed will make them feel a bit more in control, and will likely let them relax a little.

Rinse the ferret thoroughly in clear, warm running water. If your ferret has dry skin, you can use a gentle conditioner, or use a final rinse made from a quarter-cup of baking soda in a quart of warm water.

Once the bath is over, it's time for the most fun part of the project, drying off! Some people put a couple of towels and the ferret together in a cardboard box, crate, or small garbage can and let him dry himself. Others keep the ferret in a towel at chest-level, holding his head and

Ferrets will enjoy wrestling with a bath towel to dry off. To some, this is the best part of taking a bath.

Your Outta Control Ferret

torso in one hand while drying him with the other. Once you've got him mostly dry, put him back in his cage or in a smaller, confined, warm area with a dry towel to roll in, and he'll finish the job himself.

There are special "ferret dry sacks" on the market made from a water-absorbing material, with a drawstring netting across one end. You literally tie your ferret inside the bag and let him dry himself, then open the drawstring and "let the ferret out of the bag."

You'll quickly notice that a damp ferret seems to lose all sense of judgment, apparently thinking that everything *except* the towel or blanket is water-absorbent. Don't think you've damaged his little psyche when he goes racing around the room, bouncing into and off of everything in sight. . .this is simply a normal ferret's reaction to the stress of the bath, the relief that it's over, and the feel-good feeling of being clean and dry again.

In damp or cold weather, you can try drying your ferret by using a hair dryer set on its coolest setting. But be warned, only the very calmest and most confident ferrets will stand for the noise and the feel of the warm air blowing across their fur.

Nail Care

Although you won't have to make an appointment at the nail salon to get your ferret's nails done, it is important that you keep his nails trimmed short. Bath time is an excellent time for nail trimming. Most ferrets don't enjoy this procedure, but after a few wrestling bouts, most will learn to give in and accept, if not enjoy, the attention.

Ferrets are burrowers. This means that in their natural habitat, thousands of years ago, they were digging constantly. This continuous

Ferrets need to have their nails clipped regularly. If you are not sure how to do this, ask your veterinarian to show you.

digging caused their front nails to grow quicker than their hind nails. While they no longer have the need to dig, their genes still "remember" the need to grow the front nails. This means that because of their physiology, the nails on their front feet will typically be trimmed three times as often as the ones on their hind feet.

When nail trimming, keep a tasty vitamin treat on hand. Although these vitamins were originally designed and marketed for use in dogs for added luster in their coats and to encourage appetite, they have become invaluable training tools for the ferret owner who learned that the way to her ferret's brain was through his stomach.

The technique that seems to work best while trimming their ferret's nails is to hold the ferret on your lap, turn him onto his back, and drop a few drops of liquid vitamin onto his belly. When the ferret discovers his yummy tummy, he will lick himself, and be distracted from what's going on at the tips of his toes. (These oily vitamin products have the added benefit of keeping down the likelihood of hairballs in the stomach too.)

If this method doesn't work, have a helper hold the ferret by the scruff of the neck. Holding a treat, or putting a few drops of vitamin on the helper's finger will keep the ferret occupied long enough to trim the nails. Sometimes the treat may not even be necessary although you should always give your ferret a treat afterward.

Cut the nail just barely longer than the pink line inside it (This is a blood vessel, known as the "quick" and is the place where the flesh ends). Cut parallel to where the floor will be when the ferret stands, to prevent the tip from breaking off later. Be careful not to nick past that line as it will bleed a lot and your ferret will decide that he was right in the first place; that nail clipping is not a good thing! Styptic powder is handy to have around in case this happens. It will stop the bleeding quickly. You can also hold a piece of tissue or paper towel over the nail and elevate the foot for a few minutes until the bleeding stops. Placing the bleeding toenail into a small amount of sugar, or pressing it into a soft bar of soap will also aid in stopping the flow of blood. Although this bleeding will rarely be life threatening, it's a good idea to let your vet check things out if the nail continues to bleed longer than a few minutes.

If your ferret causes a fuss when you try to trim his nails, you may want to ask a helper to hold the ferret on his back.

Proper Care for Fewer Problems

Check your ferret's teeth on a regular basis. Plaque and tartar can lead to gum disease.

Dental Care

Ferrets are no different from any other pet when it comes to their teeth. They get plaque and tartar buildup on their teeth that will need to be removed to avoid decay. Just as a human gets cranky when he or she has a toothache, a ferret let you know by his behavior if he has an achy mouth.

If you gently lift the ferret's upper lip and can see dark patches on the teeth beneath the cheek, your pet needs a good dental treatment. This should be done by the vet and under general anesthesia (be sure to ask your vet to use isoflourane, as it is the anesthetic that ferrets can tolerate more easily than others) as tartar and plaque start out under the gumline, a place that a toothbrush and paste just can't reach.

Once your ferret's teeth are professionally cleaned, or if you are starting out with a very young ferret, you should start a tooth-brushing regimen at least twice a week. Use a pet enzymatic toothpaste and a small cat toothbrush. Dry kibble will also help keep the teeth clean. Ferrets that are fed only soft foods will need to have their teeth professionally cleaned more often. Normally, a ferret will need a professional dental treatment every one to three years.

Ear Care

Your ferret's ears probably won't need cleaning more often than once a month or so, at most. Dampen a cotton ball with sweet oil (made for cleaning babies' ears) or an alcohol-based ear cleaner (any ear cleaners and treatments that are suggested for cats and kittens should work well for your ferret) and gently clean them. Using peroxide-based cleaners or ointments are not recommended because wet ears are more prone to infections.

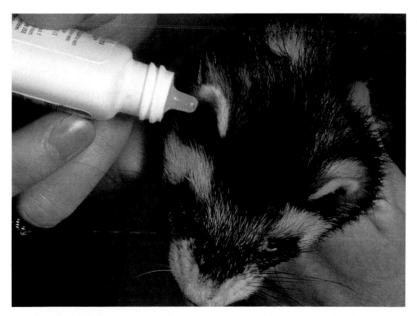

Clean your ferret's ears at least once a month. If you see dark, waxy build-up, your ferret may have ear mites. Your vet can give you medication to clear up this problem.

Proper Care for Fewer Problems

Do all you can to keep your ferret healthy throughout his lifetime. He will reward you with companionship and love.

Friends for Life

The most important aspect of being your ferret's best friend is to realize that your ferret is an individual being. He is a living, breathing creature with wants and needs and desires that go beyond simply wanting to serve and amuse his master. When those wants and needs are realized, and your ferret is accepted for simply being himself, you will have created a bond that will last a lifetime.

Holding the cotton ball along the animal's head rather than poking it straight down into the ear, will avoid accidentally injuring the ear. If you see a yellowish or brownish-red ear wax on the cotton swab, everything is normal, but if you see any black substance it means your pet probably has ear mites, which should be taken care of immediately by your veterinarian. Ear mites can make a ferret very grumpy. So if you're seeing abnormal irritability patterns, check your ferret's ears. Treatment for ear mites is simple and painless, although sometimes messy if your ferret fights the treatment.

Sleep

Ferrets are experts at sleeping. They certainly do enough of it! Once they're out of the kit stage, they are likely to sleep up to eighteen hours a day. They may always be ready to wake up and play whenever you ask them to, but they are champion snugglers and cuddlers and they love their naptimes. A ferret that is being deprived of sleep is likely to exhibit patterns of grumpiness with humans and other ferrets, and may take to showing his dissatisfaction with the situation by engaging in other bad behavior. Leave your ferret alone as much as possible while he's sleeping, and provide him with the most comfortable bedding available.

Ferrets actually need two types of beds: snuggle sacks and hammocks. Snuggle sacks (or sleepsacks) are typically a sort of bag made from a heavy-duty material, often with a fleece lining. Most have only one open end, however some are left open on both ends, creating a sort of

Ferrets sleep about 18 hours a day. You never know where you'll find your furry friend taking a nap.

Hammocks add more space to cages since they do not take up floor space. They can be strategically placed to give the ferret a "ladder" up to a higher level of the cage.

Ferrets like tents and other warm, soft places to sleep. Give your ferret an old blanket or sweatshirt to cuddle up with.

tube. They come in various sizes, for cages with single or multiple ferrets. Some sleepsack versions are unlined, but most ferrets appreciate the extra comfort found with the fleecy lining. Some types have a crinkly material liner that makes a noise, but most ferrets consider them a toy rather than a bed, although a deaf ferret certainly won't notice the difference.

Hammocks are designed from a flat piece of heavy-duty cloth, suspended from the cage walls or ceiling by chains or strings. This forms an upside-down rainbow that all ferrets love to snuggle into. Hammocks not only add more space to cages by not taking up valuable floor space, as they are suspended in mid-air, but they can be used as a sort of step to a higher level in a multiple-story cage. They can also be strategically placed so as to provide a sort of safety net in the case a ferret should fall from an upper level tray.

Just like sleep and snuggle sacks, hammocks can be lined or unlined. There are also several pocket and tube designs for hammocks that allow the ferret to sleep on the outside during warm weather, or snuggle into the fleecy interior when he gets cold.

There are also tents, "hot air balloons" and other adorable beds available for ferrets. Choose one that tickles your fancy, and your ferret is sure to agree with you.

Besides the basic hammock and sleepsacks, you'll discover the many other adorable sleeping areas on the market for your pet. Tents, igloos and wooden lodges make excellent "hidey holes" for your ferret to snuggle into if he should tire of his usual sleeping place. Keeping a wooly or fleecy blanket on the floor of your ferret's cage will also be excellent for providing a convenient cuddle for a quickie nap. There are also miniature couches, chairs and recliners available in ferret sizes, but although they look cute, most ferrets will bypass them to go to something softer, cuddlier and preferably bouncier.

Clues
to Your
Ferret's Behavior

In This Chapter You'll Learn:

✳ How to decipher clues to your ferret's bad behavior

✳ How to deal with a second-hand or rescue ferret's emotional baggage

✳ How to issue a proper correction for bad behavior

Although the ferret quite distinctly resembles its wild cousins (the weasel, the mink, and the native Black-Footed Ferret, all of which are still found in the wild in portions of the US) the domestic ferret is a separate species, and is not a "tamed wild animal" any more than is a Pekingese or a Persian cat. Thousands of generations ago a ferret might have been able to make its way in the world alone, but all those generations of domestication have made him totally dependant on his owner in today's world.

Being a devoted pet owner means more than making certain your pet's basic needs are met, it also means being somewhat of a psychologist (and having to understand your patient as he speaks to you using a

foreign language no less) when it comes to figuring out what is troubling your ferret. Once you've "ferreted" out the problem, then you have to do whatever is necessary to ensure that the problem is not only solved, but also that any previous damage done to your ferret's psyche has been repaired as much as possible.

If you know what type of environment your adopted ferret came from, it may make problem solving easier.

If you've lived with and paid close attention to your ferret for a while and know his habits well, you will notice behavior changes as they begin and perhaps be able to track down their source more rapidly. If, however, you've recently taken in a rescue animal, adopted a youngster, or added a baby to your ferret family, it may be a bit harder to track down the source of the problem. If you don't know the past history of your new ferret, don't know in what kind of situation he lived, or what he's been through that makes him act the way he does, your job will be harder.

In that case, it's time to pull out the deerstalker cape and pipe and turn yourself into Sherlock Holmes to solve the mystery. It's elementary, my dear Watson!

"The Case of the Fearful Ferret"

A ferret that has been traumatized at any age will have a hard time gaining confidence again in the types of situations that created the

When Odd Behavior is a Medical Symptom

Lethargy—Anemia, low glucose, age, heart disease, illness

Listing to one Side—Ear infection, ear mites, stroke

Walking in Circles—Stroke

Excessive Grooming—Stress, adrenal disease

Biting When Startled—Blind, deaf

Biting Other Ferrets—Blind, puberty in an un-sterilized ferret

mental or physical trauma. A young ferret may have his little psyche damaged worse than an older ferret that likely has more of an ability to "shake off" uncomfortable circumstances. Many behavior modification experts suggest using a "homeopathic" approach to working through fear anxieties, by introducing the ferret to the things

A ferret that has been scared by small children or other animals may display fear behavior, such as hiding.

that caused his fear to begin with, in very small doses, in controlled circumstances.

For instance, to calm a ferret that was scared by a larger animal, you might allow another animal to come near the ferret again for short periods of time, while the ferret is safely ensconced in his cage (his personal space, his den) allowing the ferret to realize that the animal means him no harm. After a while, take the ferret out of his cage, and introduce him to the other animal (again, in very controlled circumstances). Once he sees that there is nothing to fear, he and the animal can work on becoming friends.

A ferret that has lived with a man or woman that abused him may have developed a distrust and seemingly inordinate fear for any human of that sex. If you are of his preferred sex, and you live alone with no

Snacks

Since you will be giving a lot of treats to the ferret with a problem behavior as part of positive reinforcement training, make sure that you don't add to behavior problems by feeding inappropriate snacks. Snacks with too much sugar or not enough protein can do more harm than good. Nutritionally sensible treats that your ferret will love include meat based treats or fatty acid supplements. Cooked chicken, chicken or turkey baby foods, chicken livers, cooked egg, or chicken or turkey flavored cat treats or ferret treats will definitely tickle your ferret's fancy. A few raisins a day won't cause any problems, but they have no nutritional value for a ferret, and they do contain sugar. Avoid giving your ferret fresh fruits or raw vegetables. Large amounts of raw vegetables and fruits can cause intestinal blockages in ferrets, as they cannot digest vegetable matter.

Your Outta Control Ferret

You can give your ferret a small amount of apple as a treat on occasion, but he may be more interested in playing with it.

chance of someone of the opposite sex paying a visit or wanting to spend time with your pet, this may not create much of a problem. If, however, your ferret will likely come in contact with people of both sexes, it's important that he be gently handled by people of both sexes as often as possible. Make sure that the situation is always as controlled and positive as possible and that the person he most mistrusts has a bottomless pocket of treats!

Blindness or Deafness

Sometimes a ferret that bites out of fear may not be afraid of an actual being or situation...but rather fears the unknown. Ferrets are usually very good at compensating for deafness and sometimes even blindness. Many owners are totally surprised when their veterinarian discovers one or both medical problems.

Signs you can watch for that can indicate that your ferret is blind or deaf include the ferret not responding to loud noises, an unusual degree

A blind or deaf ferret may bite because he has been startled. Your vet can check your ferret's eyesight and hearing.

of oblivion to what is going on around him, walking into things or having difficulty navigating in unfamiliar areas. Some ferrets can fake deafness fairly well if they want to ignore your calls, and a ferret's normal sight is not up to human standards, so be sure you have your conclusions confirmed by your vet before you just assume you are correct.

A ferret that is deaf or blind will be more likely to bite their human than a ferret with normal vision and hearing. You'd bite too if you couldn't see the hands that suddenly plucked you away from what you are doing without warning, or if you heard silence instead of your human's voice telling you he was about to touch you. Almost any animal will strike out when startled, and a ferret is certainly no exception.

If you discover that your ferret is deaf or blind, don't panic. Many ferrets lead normal lives without vision or hearing. They adapt quite readily, especially if their human learns to deal with their pet's disability and creates a safe environment for them.

Fear Biting

A ferret that only bites you when you first try to pick him up might not have known you were there, and since you startled him, he was biting out of fear. Think about it. You'd bite too if huge hands plucked you up into mid-air in the middle of what you were doing.

Stopping fear biting in these cases may be as simple as making sure the ferret sees you before you pick him up. Obviously if your ferret is blind, make sure he hears or smells you before you touch him.

If deafness and blindness have been ruled out as possible factors in the aggressive behavior, you will have to delve a little deeper into your pet's psyche.

Fear Biting by the Second-Hand Ferret

If you only recently acquired the ferret that is showing signs of fear aggression and/or biting, it may be a matter of time and effort in

Many adorable, loving ferrets are in need of good homes. Consider adopting a ferret from a rescue organization.

Ferrets may bite for a variety of reasons. Try to determine what is causing your ferret to act out and remedy the problem.

gaining his confidence. Put yourself on your ferret's footpads. You've been plucked out of the only home you've ever known (even though it might not have been a *good* home, it was still *home*), packed up by strangers, moved into a new place, in a strange cage, with strange smells, sounds, and sights. You're confused and you're frightened, but instead of cowering and whimpering in the corner, you decide to show these people what you're made of, and you plan on hurting them before they can hurt you. The worst thing your new human can do is to scold you, or worse yet, hit you as a punishment for your defensive action. All that will do is enforce your belief that you are indeed in a dangerous place, and these people are really out to get you. Next time you will bite back even harder, to teach them that they're not dealing with a pussycat here. You mean business. They should leave you alone!

Eventually, if you figure out that these people actually like you, and instead of hurting you they want to give you good things to eat, scratch

Adopting an Abused Pet

There are many ferrets in the world that have never felt a caring, loving human hand in their entire lives. These ferrets will need special love and care before they will learn to trust you and realize that you have their best interest at heart. Winning their trust will be much harder than bonding with a ferret that has no reason to distrust a human. Offering your heart and home to such a ferret is admirable, and the fruits of your labors will certainly be very rewarding, but be certain that you have the time and patience necessary for the task before you make the decision to adopt an abused ferret.

your neck and your belly, keep you clean and comfortable, and give you lots of fun stuff to play with, you can calm down and decide that your new home is pretty cool. Your humans are fairly nice (and smart too ... for humans) and they don't let the other animals and noisy children bother you or hurt you. You no longer feel the need to protect yourself, so you stop biting the hand that feeds you. This makes everyone happy.

One of the best things about ferrets is that they are adaptable, but even the most adaptable animal in the world will show signs of stress when placed in an unfamiliar environment. If your ferret doesn't have any previous reason to be scared or distrustful of people, then a little patience (and a pocket filled with ferret treats) will eventually take care of this kind of problem biting.

It takes a lot of time and patience, and more than a few bandaged fingers, before an abused ferret will be willing to attempt to trust a human again. Once you've broken through that fear barrier however, you will have a bond with your fuzzbutt that most owners will never experience.

Clues to Your Ferret's Behavior

Any physical discipline on your part will most likely confirm this ferret's belief that people are out to get him, and will create even more problems. Positive training is always more effective than using negative input...certainly no pet should be hit, or yelled at for any reason, but most especially with an abused ferret you should be careful to never use any negative vocal or physical correction. Instead, reinforce the positive behavior when it occurs, and give simply a quiet, but firm, correction when he misbehaves. Soon he will learn that being good reaps rewards, while being bad may get him ignored, or put back into his cage.

Scruffing the Ferret

A good correction for a ferret is scruffing. Have you ever watched a mother animal carry her babies around? She doesn't have hands and arms, so she uses her mouth and grabs them by the loose skin at the

back of their neck (known as the scruff), and picks them up. Although some ferrets will squirm and wriggle for a moment, they will go completely limp, and most will give a big yawn. This is an excellent hold for a ferret that is a possible biter, as he will be unable to bite you while held in this position.

If your ferret has misbehaved, simply scruff him, and hold him (well away from your face) while you tell him loudly and firmly NO! Hold him there for 10 seconds or so, talking to him

Although he may protest and squirm, scruffing is a good way to let the ferret know he has misbehaved.

Your Outta Control Ferret

firmly, while explaining that he is not to bite people. Let the tone of your voice tell him more than your words.

When he has relaxed in your hold, praise him, and set him down. If he does the same thing again, react exactly the same way, with the same correction followed by praise (and perhaps a tasty treat) for behaving.

Some trainers and behavior modification experts feel that scruffing may be too threatening for a ferret that has been abused, and prefer to simply hold the ferret's head still instead. Time-outs (placing him back in his cage letting the tone of your voice express your displeasure with his actions instead of other corporal punishment) may be effective in some cases, but a ferret that was previously neglected and left shut up all the time in a lonely cage may panic if put back into his cage for a time-out. He'll see this as the very worst kind of punishment. Be lavish with praise and treats when this poor ferret is behaving well, and above all, be patient. Remember that you're only human, and leave the room when you're feeling impatient. One ill-timed flick on the nose, or impatient gesture can undo weeks of patient work and care.

"The Case of the Aggressive Ferret"

Sometimes aggression in ferrets can occur in unsterilized ferrets when they reach sexual maturity. Intact male ferrets can become so aggressive they will often kill or maim other ferrets, even females. Both sexes, when left unaltered are smellier, more aggressive, and will have more health problems. An unaltered female will stay in heat

Be Aware

It's always a good idea to contact your veterinarian when a previously sweet and happy-go-lucky ferret begins exhibiting unusual and unacceptable behavior.

Clues to Your Ferret's Behavior

until she is bred, which can cause severe anemia, and even death through the blood loss. Unless you are willing to dedicate years of your life gathering the knowledge necessary to bettering the species through selective breeding practices, there is no reason to have an unaltered ferret as a pet.

If your usually well-behaved ferret begins acting up and causing mischief, you may want to take him to the vet for a checkup.

There are many other causes for aggression in ferrets. Whenever a new ferret is introduced into their world, ferrets will fight for dominance. This fighting will continue until one ferret has established his dominance over the rest, and then life will slowly get back to normal (or as normal as life shared with ferrets can be).

Unfortunately, aggression in a formerly non-aggressive ferret may also be a symptom of an underlying health problem. Adrenal tumors, for instance, which cause overproduction of androgens, also produce an enhancement of male traits such as aggression. It's also possible that your male ferret is a cryptorchid (has one undescended testicle) that was not removed during neutering. In that case, he is technically still intact, and his behavior will change for the better after surgery to remove the hidden testicle.

"The Case of the Disappearing Owner"

Some ferrets will become so attached to their humans that their anxiety at being left behind when their human leaves home can cause startling behavior changes.

A normally sweet and gentle ferret may snap or bite when someone other than their human tries to care for it, and what is normally a hearty eater may go on a hunger strike until he is once again fed by his special someone.

A ferret that is left loose in the house, unsupervised, is a ferret on a rampage when separation anxiety strikes. The unsuspecting owner will likely come home to shredded curtain bottoms, holes in carpets and chair cushions, waste piled in corners, chewed electric cords, and overturned garbage cans. A ferret separated from those he loves is in no mood to tolerate the rules that apply when he is ensconced in his family's arms. Anything that crosses his path is fair game. Hell indeed hath no fury like a ferret that is mad at his family for leaving him behind while they are out having fun.

Some ferrets suffer from separation anxiety when they are left alone for long periods of time.

Dealing with a Lonely Ferret

To calm the frayed nerves of the ferret who does not deal well with being left alone, try getting a long-play cassette recorder, and record his favorite person's voice reading a book, or the newspaper, singing, or just cooing sweet ferret nothings into the microphone. Leave the ferret in his cage with the recorder playing when you have to leave home, and you should come home to the same quiet haven you left behind. Just make sure you arrive back home before the tape runs out.

It's a good idea to leave your ferret for very short periods of time during the training period. This reinforces the idea that even though you're leaving, you'll be back soon. When you enter the house again after your short absence, fuss over your ferret, give him a treat, and let him know how happy you are to see him. Then leave again for a little longer than before. Keep up this routine until your ferret calmly accepts your absence, and knows that your reunion will be a happy one.

It's also a good idea to have a special treat or toy that your ferret only gets to have when you're going to be gone for a while. Not only will he be so interested in his special toy or treat that he doesn't really notice you're gone, but soon he'll associate your leaving with a positive reinforcement of it being a special event, instead of the negativity of being left alone and lonely.

The biggest reward for a ferret owner is seeing a happy, well-adjusted ferret playing with his cagemates, or with his toys, oblivious to the trouble he's caused his owner with his past behavior problems. The first time a timid ferret comes running gladly to see you when you enter a room, you'll know that no matter the cost, the trouble was well worth the payoff. When you come home to find a happy fur-baby sleeping soundly in his hammock, unaware that you were even gone, much less fretting over your absence, you'll know that you and your ferret are truly

With time and patience, your ferret will become a beloved and treasured member of your household.

on the same wavelength and will be friends for life.

There's no feeling warmer than holding a ferret that once trembled and shook at any human touch, and have him gently lick your fingers or your face. When remembering the ups and downs you had while working out the house rules, and teaching him that humans are to be loved, you'll be surprised at how far you've come together. You'll feel blessed to realize how much quality time you have ahead to share.

How to Be Your Ferret's New Best Friend

In This Chapter You'll Learn:

* How to keep your ferret out of trouble (as much as possible anyway)

* How to bond with your ferret...and why bonding is so important

* How a ferret's temper can be related to temperature

* Fun games to play with your ferret

The world of a ferret is very small, even in relation to his size. It consists of his cage, the room in which he is allowed to roam freely, and occasionally, the run of your house. In his world, your influence will be all-important. He'll rely on you not only for his life's sustenance (food, water, and shelter) but also for training, encouragement, and sometimes simply to give him a silent signal that all is okay with his world. If he is frightened, he'll run to you for safety. If he is cold, he'll come to you for warmth. When he is hurt, your arms will be the ones that will offer him comfort. You will be his anchor, his hero, his guardian angel, and the only parent he will remember. And you thought when you brought him home that you were just becoming a ferret owner. Little did you know.

If your ferret finds his way into trouble in your home, consider what you can do to prevent mishaps next time.

at the adventure facing the ferret that finds himself loose inside the walls of a house.

Things that seem commonplace to you and I are intriguing beyond description to a ferret. How many times have we seen paper pulled into the printer as we print out a document, or sent a fax? We barely notice the procedure, yet to a ferret this is the equivalent of a circus sideshow act. He'll want to be center stage to watch, even if that means having to climb up the curtains to jump onto the desk, to walk across the computer monitor, to jump on the bookcase, to climb down to the shelf where he will be at risk of not only falling, but getting a toe or tail caught in the printer's rollers sending his owner careening to the vet with a bloody, loudly complaining ferret. The unsavvy owner will likely complain to her veterinarian that this darned ferret is just out of control, without giving a single thought to the fact that she should have pulled that curtain up out of his ferret's reach.

Ferrets like to dig and play in your houseplants. Some plants are toxic to ferrets and should be kept out of the ferret's reach.

Ferret-Proofing

It's important to keep your ferret's safety in mind at all times. Not all dangers are obvious. When ferret-proofing your home, get down on all fours and look at the world through your ferret's eyes. Ask yourself:

* Are all cleaning supplies and medications stored in top cabinets or in cabinets with strong childproof latches?

* Are the spaces under cabinets, stoves, refrigerators and dishwashers blocked off in the kitchen and bathroom? Are all small openings that could lead to the outside or inside the walls blocked off?

* Are the toilet lids down when the ferrets are about? Ferrets can climb into toilets while trying to drink the water and will likely drown when they can't get a toehold to back themselves up.

* Is the bar soap in an area that is out of the reach of your ferret? Ferrets can climb onto some bathroom counters and can reach the bathtub soap dish.

* Are foam rubber or soft rubber items such as hand exercise weights, shoe inserts, toys, and buckets with foam rubber handles, coasters, rubber bands or drink holders out of the reach of your ferret?

* Are all sponges and Styrofoam products in an area where your ferret can't reach them?

* Are your houseplants out of your ferret's reach?

* Do you have a "ferret safe" room in your home where your ferrets can play without constant supervision? Are your ferrets caged when you are asleep or not home?

* Are unsafe rooms blocked off with ferret-proof barriers?

* Do you always make sure your ferret is not inside a chair or couch before you sit down?

* Do you have a chair that reclines? Always make sure all of your ferrets are accounted for before you recline in it. Ferrets can easily get crushed in chair and couch springs.

Make sure that your ferret is not hiding under the couch or seat cushions when you sit down.

Give your ferret safe toys that cannot be broken into small pieces and swallowed.

* Do you check your laundry before you put it in the washing machine to make sure you're not including a sleeping ferret? Do you check the clothes dryer and dishwasher before you run them?
* Do you make sure that you keep wastebaskets with possibly harmful material out of your ferret's reach?
* Are your ferret's toys made out of hard rubber, tightly braided rope, and plastic?
* Do they play with sturdy stuffed animals that don't have small pieces that can be chewed off?

A space heater is a pretty mundane piece of equipment to most humans, but the sound of the fan turning on and off will be of utmost interest to curious ferrets. Be sure you buy space heaters that have fan-forced heat instead of heated coils that can easily cause burns to tender noses.

How to Be Your Ferret's New Best Friend

ride in your jacket hood, or to walk with you on a leash, you can spend even more time with him in the great outdoors.

Some people bond with their ferrets by holding them while listening to music or while watching their favorite TV programs. Don't give up if your ferret squirms and doesn't want to sit still with you. A tight grip (until he realizes that togetherness is a good thing), and a few tasty snacks will soon have your ferret scurrying for your lap when he sees you pick up the TV remote control.

Spend quality time bonding with your ferrets every day. They will welcome the attention and companionship.

One way to bond is to play games with your ferret. Hide a treat in a shoe and see how long it takes your ferret to find it.

Your Outta Control Ferret

Part of bonding with your ferret is occasionally reminding him that although he might appear to rule the roost, *you* are the boss. Continually training your ferret is the best way to create a bond between you. You don't have to try to teach him important things, like how to drive the family car, load the dishwasher, or bring your slippers and pipe, but you can make training a game. Train your ferret to do something simple, such as to fetch and retrieve his favorite toy for a treat. This will take quite a bit of time and effort, but will add to the bonding process.

A Fun Snack

If you're watching a movie, don't forget the popcorn! Unsalted popcorn is a great ferret treat, and they'll have as much fun playing with the kernels as they will have eating them.

Teaching your ferret to look for hidden treats is one way to keep him from becoming bored. Hide small treats in the room and let your ferret search them out.

Ferret IQ

Want to know how smart your ferret really is? Another bonding experience is trying out a few good old IQ tests. Place a treat beneath an overturned clay flowerpot and see how long it takes your ferret to not only discover the treat, but also figure out how to get to it.

Put your ferret inside a pillowcase and time him to see how long it takes him to find his way out. If you have a really smart guy, tie a very loose knot in the open end of the pillowcase to make things a little more difficult.

Toss a towel over his head, and see how long it takes him to back out from beneath it (then for kicks, drag the towel away, giving your ferret something new and fun to chase). Most ferrets will eventually grab hold of the towel and hold on for dear life as they are dragged around the floor. They can clock some pretty good speeds on linoleum or hardwood floors, although carpet does cut down on the speed somewhat.

Teaching your ferret to look for hidden treats is a fun game that most ferrets pick up quickly. Simply hide a few treats around the room and use whatever key words you choose such as "Where is it?" "Find It!" or "Who's Got the Goodie?" Soon, your ferret will begin scampering like a kid on Easter Sunday, looking for the treats his favorite friend has planted for him to find.

Fun & Games

One of the best things about being your ferret's best friend is being his favorite play partner. A bored ferret is a ferret that is going to get into trouble one way or another. A ferret with too much time on his paws is going to come up with some particularly fiendish solution to his boredom. And it's a safe bet that his solution is not one you would have

There are many ferret toys available at your local pet shop. Some ferrets like to play with crinkle sacks that make noise.

chosen to experience! Some behavior problems, such as being destructive and noisy, or repeated litter box accidents, cease when a ferret is provided with enough entertainment to not only keep him busy, but get him tired enough to want to sack out for a long nap.

There are literally thousands of games you can enjoy with your ferret, and unlike our games that require computers, CDs, expensive racquets, or other paraphernalia to play, ferret games require little beyond good human creativity, and a few household items.

Here are a few game suggestions from ferret owners around the globe. Please note that many of these games you won't even have to join, you can just watch. Also note that it's important to remember when choosing game pieces that you don't include anything with which a ferret could get hurt (sharp edges, etc.) swallow (nothing smaller than a ping-pong ball) or get stuck inside. (Few of these toys should be used without proper supervision, as most could become chewing disasters one way or the other.)

How to Be Your Ferret's New Best Friend

Crackle Ball: Purchase an inexpensive large plastic ball and cut several ferret-sized holes in it. (Be wary of any sharp plastic edges.) Fill the ball with cellophane or plastic shopping bags. Once the ferret is inside the ball, gently roll it across the floor. Soon he'll learn to roll himself along as he scampers through the crackly material.

A-Maze-ing Maze: Take a large cardboard box and fold scrap cardboard into triangular shapes, tape in place (creating an A-frame of sorts), and fill the box with as many as possible making a long maze pattern. Put a small treat in each triangular tube. Cut holes into opposite sides of the box, and turn your ferrets loose.

Reely Fun: Use a fishing rod and reel, with several red and white bobbers, attached to the end instead of a hook. Make sure your line is at least 20-pound test. Cast it across the room and reel in the bobbers, the toy, and your ferret.

Tubes make fun tunnels to explore and will keep ferrets occupied for hours.

Your Outta Control Ferret

Collapsing Tube: Take an old dryer tube and place one end into a leg cut from an old pair of pants. The ferrets will have fun burrowing into the pants and finding their way into the open tube, and vice versa. You may have to use duct tape to secure the pants leg to the tube if the ferret(s) become especially active.

Washer Run: Use two large suction cups and stick one to each side of a room. Thread a washer or ring on a string, and then tie the string from one suction cup to the other. Tie a string to the washer and the other end to a toy or waffle-type practice golf ball that the ferret can grab hold of (no smooth balls, etc.)

Feeling Sheetish: Fold a bedsheet half and spread out over the floor where you have laid slightly wadded newspaper and gift-wrapping cellophane. Ferrets love to dance around on this crinkly bed, and will also enjoy burrowing beneath it, where they will wage mock battles with the crinkly monsters they'll find lurking underneath.

Ferret-in-a Box: Take a small plastic shoebox and fill with shredded office or newspaper (office paper is cleaner, especially if you have white or light colored ferrets). Cut a ferret-sized hole in the lid, and snap the lid into place. This also makes a great hiding place for your ferrets while they're inside their cage. You can substitute wiffle ball or ping-pong balls for the shredded paper for play time.

A Tisket a Tasket, a Ferret in the Basket: Place a hook in the ceiling, and hang a long chain almost to the floor. From the end of the chain, hang a hanging basket (the plastic type used for plants). Glue any open weave material (such as a tea towel or cheesecloth) to the edges of the basket, creating a veil that drags on the floor. Your ferrets will enjoy climbing the material up to the basket where they can sway back and forth as they pretend to be adventurous hot air ballooners.

Ferrets like to play in baskets. They are great places to curl up for a nap when playtime is over.

Tubers: Prop one end of a five-foot section of 4″ diameter PVC pipe on your couch, and watch as they tube themselves down. You can cut small holes in the pipe so you can watch the fun, or cut ferret sized holes to give them even more fun possibilities.

Knit For Everyone: Toss your ferrets an old ball of yarn you don't plan on using in your knitting projects. They will have a great time rolling in it and trying to unwind it all.

King Kong Ping-Pong: Take strong thread and fasten a ping-pong ball to one end. Tie the thread to the ceiling, or to the top of a doorframe, leaving the ball hanging a couple of inches from the floor. It will drive your ferret absolutely nuts (the prime objective of any good ferret game).

Bobbing for Balls: Float ping-pong balls in a big bowl or dishpan filled with water. Be sure you place the bowl on a surface that you won't mind getting wet. One owner suggested floating frozen English peas in the water. The ferrets considered it a great treat, and very cooling for a hot summer day.

Suitcase Frenzy: Place an empty suitcase or duffel bag on the floor with all the pockets and secret compartments unzipped and open. For added entertainment, place a few pieces of apple, raisin or other healthy treats in the pockets (just make sure the ferrets have found them all before you zip everything back up to go into storage).

Any household item can be turned into a ferret toy. They like interesting places to hide and explore.

When Tempers and Temperatures Flare

Whether you're in a car or in your house, it's always important to remember that ferrets don't handle changes in temperature the same way humans do. Because ferrets originally lived in a cooler climate with underground burrows, they were protected from the heat, so they do not tolerate heat as well as animals that evolved in warmer climates.

A ferret that starts displaying erratic or unacceptable behavior during the summer months may simply be expressing his displeasure at being overly warm. Just as humans more easily lose our tempers when we are hot and sweaty, so will your ferret be more likely to snap when he is uncomfortably warm.

How to Be Your Ferret's New Best Friend

Ferrets seems to be most comfortable in temperatures at about 65° F but can do fine in summer temperatures up to 75°F. In temperatures above 80° however, they will begin to get uncomfortable, temperatures above 85° can cause medical problems within hours. Temperatures over 90° can be fatal within a few hours.

Older ferrets are more sensitive to heat than younger ferrets. Ferrets can survive prolonged periods of uncomfortable temperatures, but heat distress will eventually cause strain to the ferret's system. In cases of repeated heat stress, the immune system can be permanently compromised, making him susceptible to illness and disease.

The primary reason that our domestic ferrets have problems with higher temperatures is that they do not sweat. Humans perspire in hot weather, and the evaporation of that sweat helps cool us down. Ferrets aren't capable of doing this. They do not pant as dogs do to move air over the moisture in their mouths to cool themselves. By the time a ferret begins

Brushing away excess hair will help keep your ferret cooler in the warm summer months.

Your Outta Control Ferret

Make sure that your ferret has access to cool, fresh water at all times. Ferrets can quickly overheat in hot weather.

to pant, he is in serious distress and in danger of severe heatstroke. Immediate and drastic measures should be taken to bring his body temperature back down to the normal range. Remember to cool the ferret's body down steadily, but slowly. Don't suddenly plunk your ferret into icy water, as the ferret could easily continue the downward spiral even after he reaches the goal temperature, and could end up in worse distress than from the heat. After his body temperature has returned to normal, let your veterinarian check him out to make sure no lasting damage was done.

If your home is air conditioned, it should be easy to keep your ferret comfortable on hot summer afternoons. If you live in a warm climate, and your house is not air conditioned, keep a close eye on the heat index. As the temperature rises, take measures to ensure that your ferret stays cool and comfortable.

How to Be Your Ferret's New Best Friend

Since ferrets don't sweat, you can spray them with water to create a "fake sweat" that will cool them as it evaporates. Keeping a fan blowing on them will only help if there is moisture, as a fan doesn't actually create cool air, it only moves air around. To humans who are sweating, that makes their skin feel cooler, but this will have no effect at all on a dry ferret.

If you aren't going to be home all day to keep spritzing your ferret with water, you can place a damp towel over the top of the cage and put a bucket of water on top of that towel. Take another damp towel and place one end of it in the bottom of the bucket and the other end on the cage towel. The bucket towel will act as a wick to draw the water from the bucket, and keep the towel that is covering the cage wet. The evaporating water keeps the cage cooler. In this situation, having a fan blowing on the cage will help the evaporation (and thus the cooling) process.

You can also fill two-liter soda bottles with water and freeze them. Once they're frozen, pull a large tube sock over them and knot the end. Place the bottle in the bottom of the ferret's cage where he can snuggle against it to stay cool. Don't let a fan blow directly on the frozen bottle. You don't want to actually blow the cool air away from your ferret.

Routine Behavior

Maintaining a routine for your ferret's care is important. While you don't want to lock him into a routine so completely that he will be stressed if there is any variance at all, he will appreciate knowing that some things in life will remain the same no matter what.

It's not uncommon for ferrets to become so closely in tune to their human's schedule that they get excited at the exact time their owner is usually home from work. Always make sure you say hello to your ferret

Play with your ferret every day. Keeping a routine will let your ferret know that all is well with the world.

when you enter the house, or especially his room. If you follow any kind of schedule at all, it will be heartwarming to find him anxiously watching the door, awaiting your arrival.

It's very important to keep things as normal as possible in your ferret's little world. While they do enjoy change, it's the small changes: a new toy, new hammock or sleep sack, or chew treat that they enjoy. They don't like major upheavals such as remodeling, rearranging furniture, or, heaven forbid, actually moving into another home.

A ferret whose world is suddenly unfamiliar, even for small reasons that you or I might not consider Earth-shattering, is a ferret that will be looking for a way to make his unhappiness known. And you can bet that what he comes up with will not be something you will consider pleasant or charming behavior!

How to Be Your Ferret's New Best Friend

Your ferrets deserve the best care you can give them. Keep them safe and happy in your home and they will reward you with a lifetime of love.

If you do have to move, make sure to arrange everything in the ferret's new room as much like the old room as possible, at least until he has had a chance to become accustomed to the things you cannot recreate. Place his cage near a window if that's where you had located it in the last house. If he had a floor lamp beside his cage there, make sure he has one in the new house as well. The little things you keep in mind to make your ferret more comfortable will go a long way toward maintaining his good behavior.

Being your ferret's best friend means going the extra mile to consider his feelings in all decisions that might even remotely affect him.

How to Socialize Your Ferret

In This Chapter You'll Learn:

✳ How to introduce one ferret to another ferret

✳ How to keep a multiple-ferret household happy

✳ How to socialize your ferret with family members and other pets

✳ How to travel with your ferret

Proper socialization procedures can prevent (or cure) many perceived behavior problems. Your ferret will be more eager to please you by getting to know and interact with the people and other pets that you care about if he is truly integrated as part of your family. As stated earlier, ferrets are definitely not meant to be just 'caged animals' to sit and watch from a distance, the way you would enjoy an aquarium filled with colorful fish.

Your ferret will be happiest when he's allowed time to run and play (in a safe and secure area) and be with his family. A ferret is not a pet that will tolerate living in a totally enclosed environment, only having his food and water freshened daily, and his litter pan cleaned when

Ferrets from the same litter or family will generally get along fine together.

necessary. They are social creatures that crave attention. They will repay the attention tenfold with love and total devotion...and they'll repay neglect with an equal amount of effort. Many deeply ingrained behavior problems began as a cry for attention. Even negative attention is better than none at all to a lonesome ferret.

Ferrets are very community-oriented animals. If possible, place their cage near a very active area of the household, where they can not only get acquainted with the animals and humans that frequent your home, but where they can feel like part of the family, even during the times when they're not allowed outside their cage. This will also encourage you to keep their cage cleaner and more pleasant for them, if you're in constant contact with the odors and clutter.

Most ferrets are so inquisitive that they will enjoy meeting not only new people, but other animals as well. While most people fear that their ferret will either harm or be harmed by their other pets, there's a good

Start out slowly when you introduce two ferrets to each other.

chance that they will in fact become fast friends... if the introduction is handled correctly. An added bonus in the cross-species interaction will be the entertainment value you'll receive when your cat or dog starts playing ferret games!

When introducing your pets to the ferret (and vice versa), it is of ultra importance that you very strictly supervise the initial meeting. It's a good idea to have your dog on a leash, or your cat firmly held until you can gauge the pet's reaction to this new musky smelling interloper to their territory. No matter how well your pets seem to get along, they should never be allowed together when they're unsupervised. The most well meaning dog can easily get too involved with a game of chase or wrestle, and accidentally wound or even kill his ferret friend. Once the games start to get too rough between your ferret and other pets, it's time to have a "time-out" until all parties have calmed down somewhat. If the initial introduction is handled correctly, your pet household will run smoothly and provide hours of entertainment for you as you watch their antics. After all, who needs a TV when there's a ferret in the house?

How to Socialize Your Ferret

Dos and Don'ts for Introducing Ferrets to Other Family Pets

* DO restrain both animals until you're certain they each are aware of the other and neither is showing an inordinate fear or aggressiveness.

* DO be prepared to immediately separate the two at the first hint of discontent on the part of either pet.

* DO be especially careful if you're trying to introduce your ferret to a member of the rodent family. Because ferrets were specifically bred for many years to be rodent predators, any meeting between the two species could have disastrous results.

* By that same token, DO be careful when introducing your ferret to a breed of dog that was bred to hunt smaller animals. Sometimes hunting breeds and hounds have a tougher time adapting to thinking of a ferret as a playmate, instead of a plaything or prey.

* DON'T rush either animal into being friendly. Never shove the two together, or attempt to force them to interact. Although a dog may quickly adapt to the new member of the family, most cats like to take their time.

* DON'T neglect the old pet in favor of the new ferret. Jealousy can create rivalries that will last a lifetime and can end in bloodshed or death to the smaller of the pets.

* DON'T leave your pets unattended until you absolutely certain there are no conflicting personalities. Even then, it's best to always keep a watchful eye when your ferret is loose with other animals.

Adjusting to His New Life

Before you start filling in your new ferret's social calendar, you should take time to assess his likes and dislikes. If he has already shown an avid dislike or fear of other animals, you'll have to work up his confidence a bit before tossing him into a new relationship for which he may not be ready. If, however, he is at the front of his cage,

Ferrets may wrestle for dominance when they first meet. This is normal behavior.

with a paw extended trying to play with the dog's nose or the cat's paw, there's a good chance that you could be witnessing the start of a beautiful relationship.

If your ferret cowers in his snuggle sack or cringes in the bottom of his cage when he hears new voices, make certain that he is allowed to *slowly* get to know the humans who visit your home. Be careful that children (whose normally louder voices, frenetic actions, and hand movements will

Your new ferret may be nervous and tense in his new surroundings. Talk to him in a calm voice and give him time to adjust.

How to Socialize Your Ferret

likely terrorize a timid ferret) are well supervised when they're being introduced. Stress to them that to this little fuzz-butt they are not little people, but scary giants, and they should act accordingly to avoid frightening him further. Keep a canister of ferret treats handy for newcomers to offer to your ferret. It will help make fast friends for life.

If you acquired your ferret through a rescue organization, it's possible he may have had bad experiences with other animals and humans in the past. Some experiences may have warped the way he sees the world and how he reacts to it. For instance:

* A ferret that has been chased by a too-exuberant dog or scratched by an angry cat will be hard pressed to arbitrarily accept every new pet that crosses his path.
* A ferret that was mistreated by a child will be timid about giving another child the opportunity to hurt him again. The same goes for adults... if a male abused or neglected a ferret in a previous home, the ferret will most likely bond faster with the female in his new household, and vice versa. If you are of the gender that mistreated the ferret previously, you'll have to work twice as hard to gain his trust than would a person of the opposite sex.

Total Recall

People who spend a lot of time with ferrets are convinced that ferrets have excellent memories, especially when it comes to remembering events, people, and animals that have caused them pain. It's up to you to erase those bad memories by creating positive situations to socialize your ferret. Make him aware that life is good and that no one wants to hurt him.

Your Outta Control Ferret

Be patient and accommodating if you have adopted a young ferret. They are learning about the world for the first time.

If these little guys could talk, it would be so much easier to get to the bottom of traits that perhaps seem ridiculous and unexplainable. Who could know, for instance, that in a previous home, a child had repeatedly jumped out from behind a closet door to frighten their pet? The new owner sees a ferret that timidly approaches any open door and races for cover if a door squeaks when he's nearby. Although the new owner may suspect neglect or abuse in a previous home, he has no way of knowing how severe it was, or from what direction it came.

If your new pet came from a rescue situation, don't expect anything from him at first—instead, just provide patience and understanding and a watchful eye until your ferret can tell you in his own way what are his likes, dislikes, and fears. Then work toward a balance of acceptance on both your parts. Your ferret must learn that he can trust you, and you must learn that there will be some aspects to his behavior that you cannot change.

How to Socialize Your Ferret

Congratulations, it's a Boy (or Another Girl)

Owning a ferret is like eating potato chips—it's extremely difficult to stop with just one. You can easily justify the addition of a second ferret by saying that your first ferret needs a companion. But, just because your ferret is lonesome and you want to make him happy, don't expect him to automatically fall in love with the new friend you choose for him. Since it's usually not possible to allow your ferret to choose his own friends, it's likely that it might take some time before he accepts this newcomer that you have chosen for him. He may see this new ferret as a threat to his place on the totem pole of your affections.

Introducing your ferret to another ferret should be handled no differently than with any other animals you'd introduce. You should choose a time when you can provide total supervision for several hours. It is never a good idea to toss two animals, even of the same species, into a room or cage and let them "sort things out." Many an intense hatred was borne from such a situation, when a special friendship could have just as easily been forged under different circumstances, if handled correctly.

In a short period of time, your two ferrets will become fast friends.

Quarantine your new ferret to make sure he is healthy before you let your ferrets play with each other.

Properly introducing the two ferrets can create a bond that will last throughout their lifetimes, and not only will their lives be enriched by their closeness, but yours will be enriched as well as you watch their antics. Don't think that because you have two ferrets, however, that they will no longer need as much interaction time with their humans. Each ferret is still very much an individual, with individual needs and wants and desires.

Because there are so many illnesses that one ferret can transfer to another, it's important to keep the new ferret caged in a separate room for a few weeks. This will also give you time to bond with him on an individual basis. Once this "quarantine period" has passed, move the new ferret's cage adjacent to your current ferret's cage. This will give them a chance to get used to each other's presence and scent. Take some of the used bedding from each cage, and put it in the other. This will also help the ferrets become accustomed to the other's scent.

How to Socialize Your Ferret

After the ferrets have sniffed each other, and playfully interacted through the cage wires for a few days, it's time to introduce them to each other "up close and personal." Don't put one ferret in the cage with the other at the beginning. This will establish a false dominance for the ferret that "owns" the home turf, which isn't fair to the other ferret. Instead, close the doors to the room where the cages are, and open the cage doors, allowing the ferrets to come and go as they please. This will allow them to check out each other's cage, as well as feel as if they are making their own decisions in the matter. Hopefully, soon they'll be jumping and playing and racing around the room clucking happily, and thrilled at finding a new friend.

Wrestling Matches

Don't be surprised or upset if the ferrets start to wrestle. Ferrets have the same "pecking order" in their social groups as most other animals. Wrestling helps establish a ferret's place in his group. The ferret that is the most adept at establishing dominance (usually the male in a

Give your ferrets time to get to know each other on neutral ground.

Do not be alarmed if your ferrets wrestle with each other. They are trying to establish dominance.

male/female pair, or the larger of the two in a same-sex pair) will usually bite the other ferret on the neck, and try to drag him across the floor (amid much tumbling, twisting, and hissing). Although the first impulse of a caring pet owner is to separate the two, it's important that you allow them to work through this themselves. If the tugging becomes serious, and you truly fear for the more submissive ferret's safety, try to create a diversion to draw the dominant ferret away, giving the other ferret a chance to regroup and perhaps prepare a better defense for the next wrestling match. You can establish your own dominance and alpha status, and thus diminish the dominant ferret's confidence, by taking him by the scruff of his neck and gently dragging *him* across the floor.

If after a while, the two have done nothing but wrestle, it's best to put them back into their respective "corners" (their cages) and wait a few hours before trying again. In time, things will balance out and they'll start playing together instead of constantly seeking that pecking order.

It Takes Time

It Takes Time

Remember, proper initial introductions can take a few days (or even a few months).

If the less dominant ferret seems to constantly be trying to get away from the other ferret (and watch to make certain that this isn't some sort of "ploy" and he doesn't come back for more attention once he's left alone by the other), if he is screaming in pain, or if one of them actually bleeds, you may have to keep them separated for a longer period of time before trying to introduce them again.

Be patient during the introduction period. Taking your time now and letting them get to know each other well before they start sharing a cage will save time in the long run. It's easier to start with good behavior than to try to change bad behavior later.

If, after a reasonable length of time has passed, and your ferrets are still fighting when they're together, try putting a drop of liquid vitamins on

Proper ferret introductions don't happen overnight. The process may take several weeks or months. Be patient with your pets and let them adjust at their own pace.

Your Outta Control Ferret

Extra Love

If your current ferret sees the new ferret as a threat, or as an intruder in his space, you should spend extra time with the first ferret. Reassure him that he is still of utmost importance to you and the new ferret is not there to take his place. Give him lots of extra treats as well as extra attention. Remind him that he was there first and he will always be special to you. If your ferret is elderly or ill, it's best to choose an older ferret as a companion, or perhaps wait until your first ferret has passed on before bringing another ferret into the household.

the new ferret's head. Hold both ferrets in your arms and let your original ferret lick the new ferret. Then, reverse the procedure, allowing the new ferret to lick the original ferret's head. This not only encourages a good grooming behavior, but will help them get used to the scent and taste of the other ferret in a positive situation instead of their usual dominant/submissive posturing.

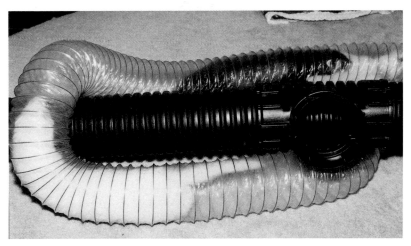

In time, your ferrets will learn to play nicely together. These ferrets enjoy chasing each other through this plastic tubing. Be sure to give each of them individual attention every day.

How to Socialize Your Ferret

Only allow your ferrets to share a cage when they have consistently played nicely together, or slept together outside their cages. Even then, it's best to cage them together only briefly, and only when you are home, for at least the first few days. Just keep your ears open for sounds of fighting, and check them over frequently for signs of injury.

And Baby Makes Four…or More

It is of utmost importance to help your ferret adjust to the arrival of a new human baby by preparing him for the upcoming event ahead of time. It's not fair to a ferret, any more than it would be to a young child to suddenly have them awakened by strange sounds and smells and a new creature in the household, vying for attention that was formerly all theirs.

Young ferrets are extremely sensitive to change. If you are expecting a child, be sure to give your ferret extra attention and introduce the new changes in small increments. A new toy could ease your ferret's concerns.

Ferrets and Babies

It's not a good idea to leave your ferret alone with a newborn baby, no matter how well trained or well mannered the ferret may be. The quick kicks and hand wavings that babies make can be startling to a ferret, and he might snap or bite without meaning to do damage. The ferret's teeth are sharp enough to inflict damage to delicate baby skin.

While it's easy to overlook this task when you're getting yourself and your home ready for the blessed event, you can make gradual adjustments to your lifestyle before the baby arrives that will help your pet handle his confusion, anxiety and jealousy when the time comes.

Ferrets are very sensitive to sounds and smells and they use this very special ability to gather information and make determinations about what is a supposed threat and what is acceptable. Your pet will have established the "normal" smells and sounds for you and your home. He'll also be very aware of your moods as well as your different tones of voice and your body language.

The addition of a new baby, especially in a house that had previously been home to only adults and pets, will have what will seem to a ferret to be startling differences in everything he thought he knew about his home. Different sounds will startle him from sleep. Different smells will assault his senses when he roams the house. His humans will be acting differently than he has ever seen them act. Just as a young child would be confused and would act out his confusion and fears with misbehavior, so will your ferret demand attention and reassurance by using bad behavior.

How to Socialize Your Ferret

New Smells

Aside from the sounds a new baby makes, the smells that accompany it can range from disgusting to intriguing to a ferret. Before the baby arrives, put baby lotion, baby powder, and baby food on your clothes or skin, and let the ferret get used to the mingling of those smells with your own personal scents. Perhaps a friend will let you "borrow" a dirty diaper, so you can let your ferret become accustomed to that smell as well.

If your home is a noisy household with people and pets constantly traipsing in and out, phones and doorbell constantly ringing, and a TV or stereo blaring loudly, it's likely that the sounds a baby makes won't be quite as upsetting to your ferret as they might be to a ferret who is used to living in a quiet atmosphere. Find or make a recording of baby cries, gurgles, and other noises, and play it for your ferret while feeding treats or during playtime. Reassure him if he appears upset, and praise him if he expresses curiosity, or better yet, shows acceptance. Remember to smile while you're reassuring and praising him. It makes a difference in the tone of your voice, and your ferret will quickly realize that these new sounds make you very happy and he will more likely be accepting.

Once you've brought your baby home, be careful to not speak to your ferret in negative tones when the baby is in the room. A continuous litany of "No!" "Off!" "Don't!" and "Stop!" will make your ferret connect unhappy feelings with the presence of the baby, and make him resentful of the baby's presence. Make the time the ferret spends with the baby a pleasant time. Always have treats handy to share with the ferret when the baby is getting a bottle or food. Be sure you continue to spend quality time with your pet, even if it is time that has to be shared with the baby as well.

Your Outta Control Ferret

Once your ferret has been carefully introduced to every member of the household from children, to pets, to parents and neighbors, he is ready to become a productive member of society by attending family meetings, spending time with family members and pets, and even traveling with you when you visit other households. Proper socialization will make all the difference in the way your ferret looks at the world ... and the way the world looks at your ferret.

Traveling with Your Ferret

As with most friends, you may find you want to take your ferret along on road trips. Although your ferret isn't going to be much help when it comes to watching for highway markers or helping to read the road map, he can be excellent company for you on long rides.

Ferrets love going places. You can fix up a carrying case with a litter pan and a space for food and water, and take your pet with you wherever he is welcome.

Car trips don't seem to bother ferrets, and most will complain more loudly about being confined into a smaller travel cage than the movement of the automobile, or the stopping and starting movements. Never let a ferret loose in the car however, since they can easily get beneath your feet causing an accident if you need to accelerate or brake rapidly. They can also "ferret" their way through a hole in the dash, and make their way through the engine compartment and onto the road.

Flying with a Ferret

A few airlines will allow ferrets to be carried onto a plane in under-seat carriers as 'carry-on luggage.' Although most airlines will allow ferrets to be shipped in the cargo area, this isn't recommended just for pleasure trips. As careful as airlines try to be to ensure our pet's

A secure pet carrier, such as the Fold-Away Pet Carrier by Nylabone®, will keep your ferret safe while traveling.

comfort during travel, you have to realize that if cargo was a really pleasant place to ride, they would put seats down there and sell tickets to humans. Cargo shipping can be used in case of emergency, or during a move where not doing so would mean having to find a new home for your pet. Be sure that whichever way you ship your ferret, you get approval in writing. One person in the ticket office may say it's okay, only to have you show up to ship your ferret only to find someone else on duty who says they're not accepted.

Tranquilizing your ferret for travel is not recommended unless the trip is an absolutely necessary one, and your ferret has proven himself to not be a good travel candidate. Ask your vet about proper tranquilization practices, and follow their instructions (and their warnings) to the

Warning!

Some ferret owners, (although they likely won't admit it) get a thrill out of carrying their ferrets into places where the ferret would not be welcome. Although this is a harmless practice in many cases, **never** take your ferret into an eating establishment, or into any public place when you're in a state that considers ferret ownership illegal. You could be literally endangering your pet's life in the case of accidental discovery.

letter. Never attempt to use other medications to make your pet drowsy. Remember he's going to be unsupervised for several hours and no one would be around to help in case he goes into distress.

Ferrets in Hotels/Motels

If you're staying at a hotel during a trip, be sure to warn the management (and housekeeping) that there will be a ferret in the room. Be prepared to pay a non-refundable deposit for the privilege of having your little furry travel partner along. It's a very good idea to take along a travel cage and promise to keep the ferret inside the cage when he's in the room. Even the most well-behaved ferret can have accidents when in a strange location, or he can lose his mind with the heady intoxication of the scents left behind by previous occupants, causing even a usually non-destructive ferret to do damage to hotel property.

Remember that you and your pet will be considered ambassadors for every person who follows after you with his or her pet, so please be on your best behavior. Don't allow your ferret to roam loose in the hotel room unsupervised. Be honest and tell the management about any accidents or damage, and offer to make restitution. You can't blame hotels and motels for refusing to welcome people traveling with their pets if they are continually met with undesirable "gifts" after pets have departed the premises.

Some ferrets like to travel. If you bring your ferret into a hotel or motel, keep him in his travel crate or pet carrier when you are not there to supervise him.

How to Socialize Your Ferret

Traveling with Your Ferret

What to bring along:

Proper Paperwork: Always carry proof that your pet has been vaccinated for rabies. Most campgrounds and parks will not let you in without proof of shots and a valid rabies certificate.

Identification: Ferrets are likely to become very nervous in strange environments. Be sure your pet has on an ID tag in the unlikely event of his running away. This tag should have your name and a phone number of someone (a neighbor, your vet, another family member) who can reach you while you're traveling.

Food and Water: Always carry a supply of ferret food when you travel. Don't count on being able to find your normal brand in other parts of the country. Be sure it's kept in a well-sealed container and feed a little less while traveling, due to the possibility of upset stomachs. Water is also very important, since stress can easily cause a ferret to become overheated when riding in a car.

Litter Pan: Although hopefully you'll be able to give your ferret nice long walks along the way (since he's so well-trained now that he loves walking on his leash) it's unlikely he'll want to spend precious exploration time attending to business, so it's a good idea to purchase a small litter pan that will fit in his travel cage.

Toys and Bedding: Take along some of his favorite toys, and bedding that he's had in his cage at home. Both will make him feel more secure and help him realize that you are a common denominator in all situations in his life. Wherever you are, is home.

Just as none of us want to step in dog waste when we take a walk around the motel grounds, so will the maid (or the next guest) not be happy to find ferret surprises hidden in the closet, or beneath the bed, or to discover chewed furniture, nibbled phone cords, or shredded bedding. Be a good ambassador. Make your ferret a model guest, and pave the way for those who follow you.

Miscellaneous Travel Tips

1. Don't feed your ferret for two to three hours before you leave home. Feed sparingly while on the road to avoid upset stomachs.

2. Make sure your ferret can see outside from his crate, and keep a window cracked open so he can get fresh air while in the car.

3. Never leave any pet unattended in a vehicle, even if he is securely ensconced in his crate. During summer months, temperatures inside a car (even one with windows left partially opened) can quickly escalate to life threatening ranges. If you know you will have to be away from the vehicle during your trip, leave your pet at home.

Ferrets and the Law

If you're going to be crossing state or country borders, make sure what the law says in relation to ferrets *before* you arrive at a border crossing. Be prepared to have distemper and rabies vaccination proof in writing to show to any border authorities. Be aware of what states consider ferrets illegal, and which ones have the written authority to confiscate and put your ferret to death. Obviously, ferret lovers should avoid those states at vacation time. Consider spending your tax dollars in states that show common sense in their animal legislation.

Why do some states have such stringent legislation? Lack of proper research on the part of legislators is something that is being addressed in most states by avid ferret supporters who realize the inappropriateness of the laws. Most of these laws were passed because of the popular misconception that ferrets pose a serious rabies danger, when in fact, studies have indicated that it's not only hard for a ferret

Some states make it illegal to keep ferrets as pets. If you take your ferret out of your home state, be sure to have proof of vaccinations with you.

to catch rabies, but when one does, it dies very quickly, so the danger to humans is very small.

Another supposed reason for banning ferrets is the idea that escaped pets will form feral packs and threaten livestock or native wildlife. There are no confirmed cases of feral ferrets in the US, and the few deliberate attempts to introduce domestic ferrets to the wild have failed miserably, so this, too, is an unfounded fear.

Play it Safe

Always keep your ferret closely confined when you're away from home. Having a lost ferret is terrible enough when you're on your home turf. In strange surroundings, it can create overwhelming problems. Carry a photograph of your ferret with you in case he is lost and you have to create "Lost" posters. This can also be used as identification and proof of ownership if he is turned into a shelter. Keep a lightweight collar on your ferret at all times during travel, complete with an identification tag, and a bell. The bell might help you find him, and the ID tag will help the finder contact you (don't include your home phone, remember, you're not home, you're on vacation... instead use that of your vet or a neighbor or relative).

Your vacation can be greatly enhanced by the presence of your little furry best friend. You'll be amazed at the new friends you'll make along the way when you're out walking with him at rest stops. You can be a great ambassador for the species by having your healthy, well-trained, happy ferret eagerly greet new people. You'll help prove that the stereotypical weasel-like creature is a far cry from the pet that can share your heart and home if you're willing to get inside his mind and truly become his best friend.

Watch your ferret closely and do all you can to prevent escapes. Make sure your ferret wears a collar and identification tag at all times. It will help you find your pet if he becomes lost.

How to Socialize Your Ferret

Riding with Your Ferret

Taking your ferret for car rides can be a bonding experience, if you train him to enjoy them. Although most ferrets adapt quite happily to traveling, there's nothing quite so headache-inducing as listening to the non-stop, piteous whimpers of an unhappy ferret "trapped" in a vehicle.

There are several reasons why your ferret might not enjoy a trek through the neighborhood. First, the car vibrates, throwing off his equilibrium, and it makes scary noises. Although the ferret might enjoy the novelty of the feelings and sounds if he was inside his "safe zone" (cage/room) it's a different ballgame when he's in unfamiliar surroundings. Second, the ferret can't see what's going on around him, since the cage is usually sitting on the floor of the car or in the back seat, and thus too low for him to see out a window. Third, many times the only car rides the ferret has taken have ended badly. Car rides mean going to the veterinarian's office, or are a precursor to a change of home, or some other equally unpleasant indignity. Think about it, if every time you got into a car and it took you to your annual doctor's exam, how excited would you be to hop in?

The first thing to do when setting out for a ride is to raise your ferret's cage or travel carrier to a level so he can see out the window. Being able to see outside will give your ferret a greater sense of security, and the strange sounds and sensations won't bother him quite as much. Putting a couple of pillows beneath the travel crate or cage will not only lift the cage higher, but will act as shock absorbers to lessen the vibrations. Use a shoulder seat belt to secure the carrier so it doesn't topple off the seat. This will also keep your ferret safer in case of a car accident.

Now that he can see outside, give him a view he'll enjoy. Think about how bored he must get seeing the same things over and over every day.

No wonder it doesn't take much to send him into those displays of wild abandon that leave the room in chaos.

We get to leave the house and go out into the world alone, we watch TV and videos, and our world is endless. Your ferret's world stops

at the door. While you might enjoy sitting with him while you watch *Quigley Down Under* a few dozen times, chances are that he'll miss the plot of the movie every time. Your ferret friend would much prefer sitting in his travel cage in a quiet area with trees and birds and other animals for him to watch.

As you drive, open the window an inch or two so he can smell the fresh air and get the full experience of all these exciting new things. Don't make the first outing very long, and give him lots of treats throughout the trip. If you're going to be gone for very long, you'll need to include a litter pan in the travel cage.

It may take a few of these short just-for-fun drives before your pet learns to look forward to them. Take trips every few days to reinforce the memory. Once a week or so after that will keep your ferret rarin' for adventure, and he'll run excitedly to you when he hears the car keys rattling.

How to Socialize Your Ferret

Practical Solutions to Outta Control Problems

In This Chapter You'll Learn:

✱ How to deal with biting and nipping

✱ How to curb chewing and digging

✱ How to housetrain your ferret

M ost ferret breeders have gotten many a call from a frantic pet owner who has suddenly become afraid to play with, or sometimes even handle their ferret. Getting your ferret to stop biting can be a simple procedure—if you are patient and understanding, and consistent with your training (or re-training) methods. First you must understand why your ferret is biting. There are many reasons other than simply a bad temperament.

Fear

A ferret that bites is very often just afraid, and is not a ferret with a bad personality. Remember to look at the world from the ferret's point of view: he was taken away from mom and siblings when he was just a few weeks old, had major surgery, was shoved into a box, flown in a scary

Training

One way to be your ferret's best friend is to spend time training him. Although your ferret isn't going to retrieve the daily paper, or be able to enter a dog obedience ring any time soon (even if the AKC would allow them) he is smart enough to learn to sit up, turn around, roll over, sit on your shoulders, ride in your jacket hood, and even walk on a leash. The biggest trick in training a ferret to do anything is to hold his attention. Ferrets don't have the longest attention span in the world (an understatement as you'll quickly discover). It's very important to schedule your training sessions for when the quick burst of energy and exploration has abated somewhat after first being turned loose in a room, and before they get too tired to want to do anything other than sleep. With ferrets, timing is indeed everything.

Unlike dogs, ferrets won't do anything for the simple pleasure of pleasing their master. Since they believe they were put on Earth simply to enjoy life and be catered to, the concept that they owe you anything

First You Must Train Yourself

A problem in any relationship is seldom the fault of just one of the parties involved. As the old saying goes, "it takes two to tango." Many times you'll discover that something you have done (or not done) is the reason behind your ferret's behavior problem, or at least has reinforced the problem. Owner error is the most common reason for a ferret's problem behavior, as it is the true nature of the ferret to be happy, good-natured, and want to please his humans. Understanding ferret psychology, and then learning to interact properly with your ferret will ensure the two of you have a long, happy, and productive friendship that will happily span the years.

Your Outta Control Ferret

is beyond the simple comprehension of most ferrets. Although they may adore you, the idea of wanting to please you will be foreign to most. After all, isn't just having them around reward enough for you? Why should they do something they don't really want to do, just because you want them to do it?

Training Rewards

It's important to remember the old adage that the way to someone's

heart is through the stomach, and the same is true to the way to a ferret's brain. Want them to perform a trick? Teach them that when they've performed correctly they get a treat. Such positive reinforcement is the only correct method for training a ferret. You should never hit any animal during training, correction, or for any other reason. A ferret won't learn anything except hate or fear if you use negative reinforcement such as spraying him with water, swatting him with a paper, throwing a shoe at him, or any other type of physical abuse. Always accentuate the positive.

To put it even more simply, do not show any reaction to behavior that you do not like, but lavish attention on behaviors of which you approve. The trick is to always be consistent with your training (and insist that other family members that work and play with your ferret follow the same rules), and although you won't see a change in behavior overnight, you'll soon notice that your ferret is making a conscious effort to do the things he knows will please you, instead of exhibiting previous problem behaviors.

Practical Solutions to Outta Control Problems

One of the most important things to teach your ferret is to be amenable to being restrained, either by a leash, or by sitting on your shoulders or riding in the hood of your jacket. Training him to a leash is the simplest...just put the harness in place and let him get used to wearing it indoors, while dragging the leash around behind him (only do this when you were there to supervise in case the leash becomes entangled and your ferret becomes trapped). Once he stops fighting this alien attachment, you can venture into other rooms in your house, and finally out into the great outdoors. Don't expect your ferret to learn to heel like a dog. Walks with a ferret rarely go in a straight line, or where you wanted to go. Learn to deal with it, realizing that these forays are for the ferret, not for you.

Teaching a ferret to ride on your shoulder or in your hood is a little harder than walking on a leash, but it's not rocket science either. Simply stand over a pile or basket of crumpled newspaper with your ferret on your shoulder. When your ferret falls off your shoulder into the soft

Come, Please

Another very important trick to teach your ferret is to come when you make a particular noise (a whistle, a kissing noise, or even clapping your hands) or squeak a particular toy. Make the noise each time before you give the ferret a treat for a while, then make it when your ferret isn't nearby and give the treat as a reward when he comes to you. Ferrets often won't respond to their names, and it's enormously helpful to have a way to call your pet when he is out of sight somewhere. Deaf ferrets can be trained to come by using a flashlight and blinking it off and on rapidly for a strobing effect (even some hearing ferrets will actually be trained easier to visual cues such as a strobing light, rather than a sound).

With time and patience, you can train your ferret to walk on a leash. Be sure to buy a secure, escape-proof ferret harness.

landing pad, shout "No!" The combination of the fall, the noise, and your shout should persuade him to pay more attention to staying on. Give him a treat when he does, and he should learn quickly. Carry treats in your pocket whenever your ferret is riding on your shoulders as a reminder that staying in place is a good thing. (When you're outdoors, it's wise to keep a harness and leash on your ferret, preferably attached somehow to your clothing, so if he falls off your shoulder, or out of your hood, he is still restrained and won't be able to escape.)

Reinforcement

During the training process, your ferret should be rewarded (with food or other positive reinforce-ment) when he acts properly – meaning every time he doesn't bite when you pick him up. Soon, he'll learn that there's something good in it for him when he's good. Give him an incentive to

Practical Solutions to Outta Control Problems

Train your ferret to listen to your commands. Reward him when he does something right. He will quickly learn what is expected of him.

act properly, and you'll see definite positive changes in his behavior. What about when he isn't good? You should scruff him like a mama ferret would do, shake him gently, and even hiss at him if his behavior was particularly bad. He'll quickly learn that he made a mistake.

To begin training, you'll need to have a few supplies on hand. The most important is a cage (which you already have, as few ferrets are total house pets). This cage should be used during training as a place for "time-outs." You should have a ferret-proofed place for him to play outside of the cage. You'll also need a wide variety of toys a ferret can have fun with.

The most important thing to have in great supply while doing behavior modification is patience! You must have the patience to not only remind yourself that this ferret is worth the effort it will take on your part to

Your Outta Control Ferret

break this bad habit, but the patience to hold your temper and remain consistent with the training.

During the training process, there are two skills at which you'll need to become adept, as you will find that both will come in very handy in many situations when dealing with your ferret.

First is the *control hold*. This is a very useful way to learn to pick up a ferret that is prone to nipping. When this hold is used correctly, the ferret cannot bite you, no matter how hard he tries.

Food is a good motivator to a ferret or any other animal. Use food rewards as part of your training regimen.

First, make a V shape with your index and middle finger. When you pick up the ferret, his head will go back into this V, with your index finger on one side, your middle finger on the other. This leaves your thumb and other fingers free to hold onto his torso so that he cannot wriggle around and nip you. Although this may take a bit of practice, once you've got the hang of this grip you'll find that no matter how much your ferret wriggles and twists, he is virtually helpless. He can squirm all he likes, but he can't bite you. Eventually he will give up and admit defeat.

Scruffing

Next, you'll need to practice *scruffing*. Remember, scruffing is just what it sounds like. To scruff your ferret, grab the loose "extra" skin at the back of his head and neck and lift him up. You'll quickly see that he can't bite you in this position. Some ferrets will go completely limp when they're scruffed. Some will yawn in an attempt to show you they don't really care what you're doing, and others will try to squirm their way out of your grip. Just hang in there, or rather keep him hanging in there, and soon you'll impress on the ferret that not only are you bigger than he is, but you truly do have the "upper hand" in the situation.

Vocal Corrections

Whether you scruff, or use a control hold, your vocalizations are an important part of any training procedure. After a bite, tell the ferret "No" or "Stop" or whatever code word you decide to use. It's important that you be consistent with your words as well as your

Ferrets can be a handful, and many misunderstood ferrets wind up at animal shelters or rescue organizations. Be a responsible pet owner and take the time to train and socialize your ferret.

Practical Solutions to Outta Control Problems

actions, because the ferret will quickly learn the meaning of certain words. A time will come when all you need to do to stop a bite from happening is to say your code word, with no accompanying action at all.

Staying Friends

Make sure after *any* disciplinary action that the ferret knows you're still friends. In the case of a true problem biter, if the ferret comes back for more after you have scolded, scruffed, and then put him down, give the ferret a time-out in the cage until he is calm enough for you to pick up without being bitten again. It's a good idea to have a stuffed animal to put with the ferret, for him to work out his aggravation on, without putting yourself or other animals in danger of being bitten. Some ferrets have learned to work out their aggression on stuffed animals and have become model citizens with no thoughts of biting their human.

Although your ferret may bite or nip a fellow ferret in play, he should be taught never to bite a human.

Your Outta Control Ferret

Bad habits are often the result of boredom. If your ferret becomes destructive, he may be acting out because he is bored. Give your ferret a toy or channel his attention onto something positive.

Discourage Biting

Although some training books will suggest tapping the ferret's nose to discourage biting, many people feel that this is not a proper method of discipline for mustelids. If you expect your ferret to change his behavior for you, then the least you can do is try to understand his language.

To a ferret, nose flicking, tapping, pinching etc. are likely to be interpreted into ferret-ese as one of two things: you are willing to play as rough as he is, which will make him bite more often and harder; or, you are trying to establish a fear dominance over the ferret, in which case the ferret will become even more afraid of you, and any fear-biting will become reinforced. Many people have successfully trained their

Beating Boredom

Many animals, including ferrets, develop bad habits in response to their own boredom. For instance, many ferrets learn to tip their food bowl over when they find themselves with time on their paws. This not only sends food scattering through their cage, giving them something to chase and hide, but the action is likely to bring attention from their owner. Even negative attention is welcome to a bored ferret!

Keep lots of interesting toys in the cage for your ferret to play with and change them out occasionally so he always has something different to look forward to. Let him out of his cage for several hours daily to get a change of scenery. You may find that his behavior problems disappear when you learn to help him beat boredom!

ferrets using this method, but in the opinion of most behaviorists and trainers, you run too great a risk of damaging the ferret, either physically or mentally.

If training methods don't seem to be altering your ferret's biting habits, try using Bitter Apple (a bad tasting spray or paste available at many pet and farm supply stores) on your hands when you pick up your ferret. He'll quickly decide he doesn't like the taste of human flesh. (Just remember to wash your hands before you do any cooking, or put your fingers in your own mouth. Blech!)

It probably should go without saying that until you have worked through any nipping or biting problems with your ferret that you not allow him around other people. Be sensible if you live in an area that has a "kill and test" rabies policy for ferret bite incidents. Please be a good ambassador for the species when you warn people not to touch your ferret and assure them that it is not normal behavior for a ferret to bite.

Your Outta Control Ferret

Housetraining

Although ferrets can be trained to use a litter box, it's usually not an overnight process. Unlike cats, who have a seemingly ingrained desire to use a litter box (and cover their waste immediately) a ferret has to be trained to use his pan. It can be a challenge, but you can do it if you're willing to invest the time and effort required to do it properly. Being diligent from day one will mean you will reap the rewards from your perseverance for the lifetime of your pet.

Of course, as with any other training, you need to gather the basic equipment. You'll want to purchase several litter boxes, the main one being for a corner of the ferret's cage. The higher the sides of the pan, the better, as a ferret's "aim" is not always good. If your ferret is a digger, you may have to attach the pan to the sides of the cage, so that he can't tip the box. You can punch holes in the side of the pan and attach it with wire, bungee straps, or good old duct tape. (Most ferrets

A ferret can be litter box trained much like a cat. Be patient with your ferret until he understands what the box is for.

Keep a litter box in your ferret's cage. He will learn to use it as a bathroom in no time.

love to play in their litter box when it's filled with fresh litter, so it's a good idea to put a tiny bit of waste in the box each time you clean it, to avoid turning it into a playpen).

If you have a large, multi-level cage, you may want to put a smaller litter box on one of the upper levels if you notice your ferret having accidents inside the cage. If they're up in the "attic" playing when the urge to use the bathroom strikes, very young or very old ferrets may not have the bladder control to wait until they can jump from level to level to get down to their first floor bathroom.

Put about an inch or so of litter in the box and cover the rest of the cage floor with cuddly old t-shirts or some other comfortable bedding

The More Boxes the Better

Be sure to have enough litter boxes in any room where the ferret will be allowed to run loose and play. Very few ferrets will take the time to find their way back to the box in their cage when they get the call from nature. Notice where your ferret goes to the bathroom, (it will always be in a corner) and place a pan there. Be sure to clean all his litter pans every day.

for your ferret. With any luck, he'll use the litter box on his own. After all, the rest of the cage floor is a bed, so that only leaves the litter box for the bathroom.

Before you take your ferret out of his cage for playtime, place him in his litter box to see if he has to go. Only after you've seen him

Avoid "Accidents"

If your ferret starts to back into a corner while he's out of his cage, it means he has to go to the bathroom. Quickly put him in the box in his cage and praise him when he uses it.

eliminate should you let him out of his cage. About every fifteen minutes or so you should pick up your ferret and place him in the litter pan in his cage. If he does use his box, give him lots of praise, and a small treat.

Keep many litter boxes arranged around the room. If your ferret is not near a litter box, he may go behind a piece of furniture to do his business.

Practical Solutions to Outta Control Problems

Once you've introduced the basic concept of using a litter box, it's time to add another litter box ... outside the cage, in a corner of the play area. You can put Velcro on the bottom of the pan so it can't be easily tipped over. Be sure you place a "sample" in the new litter pan to give the ferret the idea that this is his bathroom away from home when he's outside his cage.

As you expand your ferret's territory by allowing him into other rooms of the house, always make certain to have adequate litter pans in each room. In large areas, having a pan in each corner isn't really overkill, and will likely pay for itself in time. Some ferrets might try to race to the opposite end of the room searching for their box when nature calls, but most will simply shrug and say "It's too far, and I'm busy." and head for the nearest corner.

Mistakes Happen

The key to success in litter training, as with any other training, is diligence. It's very important to supervise every moment your ferret is out of his cage until you're sure he can be trusted to find his litter pan(s). Praise every success, and quickly clean up any accidents. Using a carpet or floor cleaner specifically formulated for pet odors is a good idea, although baking soda and vinegar are both good non-toxic clean-up materials.

If you notice that your ferret has consistently chosen a corner other than the one where you've placed a litter box, try moving the box to that corner. If he then uses the corner from where you've moved the box, you can assume he's just being mischievous, and you'll have to work harder to avoid mishaps.

If you catch your ferret about to make a mistake, it's very important to quickly let him know he's doing the wrong thing. If you can catch him

Your Outta Control Ferret

before he actually "let's go" you can loudly say "No!" and then place him in a litter box. Praise him when he uses the box. If you catch him after the fact, but still in that location, and just "finishing up" you can scruff him, scold him, and put him in his cage for a few minutes of "time-out" for him to think about the error of his ways. Take some of the fecal matter and put it in the ferret's litter box to make it smell like a bathroom to him. Mistakes need to be cleaned up promptly and completely. Once the area has been cleaned, place cuddly material there so the area will seem more like a bed than a bathroom.

Correcting Mistakes

Don't bother scolding your ferret when you find an accident minutes, or even seconds later. Scolding a ferret that is on the couch in the living room playing with a toy, for messing in the corner of the bedroom is a futile endeavor. Your ferret will perceive being scolded for either being on furniture or playing with a toy. His little bathroom indiscretion will be far from his mind at that point and you'll just confuse him with your displeasure.

Although almost every ferret can be trained to use a litter pan, there will be individual variation. Frankly, ferrets just aren't as diligent about their pans as most cats are, so there will be an occasional accident.

Two ferrets will keep each other company and provide companionship for each other when you are not home.

Practical Solutions to Outta Control Problems

Buy Me a Buddy?

Sometimes when an owner is at the end of her rope when dealing with a frustrated ferret, the answer may seem to be that the ferret needs a buddy. While this may in fact help the situation if boredom is the only issue, it can also exacerbate other situations, making them even worse than they were before.

There's always the chance that the two ferrets won't get along and will have to be caged separately, which will double your responsibilities in regards to keeping another cage and complete set of supplies clean and tidy. You could end up with not one misbehaving ferret, but two ferrets with behavior problems. Then what will you do?

It's best to make an effort to co-habit happily with the one ferret you have before you double the trouble...even though admittedly, you'll be doubling the fun as well! If you decide to add another ferret to your household, check with ferret rescue organizations. There is usually a long list of wonderful ferrets eagerly anticipating a new home with a ferret buddy. Be sure to tell the rescue personnel what problems you're having with your current ferret, so you don't add to the problem by bringing in another ferret that thinks those behavior problems are normal, too.

Even well trained ferrets tend to lose track of their litter pans, particularly when they're frightened or excited, or if they're in a new house or room. At least ferrets are small, so their accidents are pretty easy to clean up.

Occasionally an older, previously well-trained ferret will seem to completely forget his housetraining. At that point, you will need to retrain him by confining him to a smaller area or even a cage for a week or so, starting over with the general housetraining practices, and gradually expanding his space as he catches on again. Remember that

A ferret will chew on anything. Make sure you ferret-proof any
room in the house where your ferret runs free.

this could also be a sign of a health problem, so keep a close eye out for
other symptoms.

Chew on This

From the moment a ferret baby's teeth pop through the gums, a ferret
is a living, breathing, chewing machine. Nothing is sacred to a ferret so
long as it will fit between his jaws. Any dangling wire (or even wires
neatly wrapped and tucked away supposedly out of sight) to a computer,
TV, lamp, or any other electrical source is fair game to a ferret with a
desire to chew. Many a TV repairman, or computer technician has been
called out on a house call from a panicked homeowner with a dead TV
or non-functioning computer, only to find a frayed and tattered wire.
Not only is this type of damage potentially expensive but it also can be
dangerous, and even fatal, to your ferret.

Practical Solutions to Outta Control Problems

Part of ferret-proofing your house before allowing your ferret "free roam" privileges should be tying all loose cords up, and attaching them firmly to the underside of furniture, out of sight and reach of a ferret.

To keep your ferret from chewing on things he shouldn't, give him lots of chewable toys and encourage him to chew on them instead. Cloth "bones" made from rope make great ferret chew toys. They are safe to chew since the small threads are made of 100% cotton and are relatively safe to ingest. Many owners have found that their ferrets like to chew on Velcro, so they provide them with a long strip of the prickly side for chewing. This works as a ferret toothbrush as well, which will help keep down dental plaque. If you find your ferret chewing something he shouldn't, scold him and distract him with a suitable chew toy. Praise him when he takes the toy and begins chewing on it instead.

Digging is a natural instinct to a ferret. They will try to dig up the corners of unsecured rugs.

Your Outta Control Ferret

Digging

The same urges and burrowing instinct that cause a ferret to chew will also cause him to dig in such places as the carpet, in the litter box, in laundry baskets or wherever the urge strikes them. While some digging isn't destructive, constant digging in one spot for long periods of time can be extremely hard on carpets, bedspreads, and upholstery.

Doorjambs and molding are other areas where ferrets like to scratch and dig. Keeping your ferret's nails clipped will help reduce digging damage.

Ferrets seem especially drawn to the area of flooring directly in front of any door. They will

Once the ferret has dug under the rug, he may continue to dig and burrow beneath it, and may even dig at the floor.

dig and dig at this spot until they have shredded the carpet, or ripped the linoleum. The sides of the door won't fare much better. Interestingly enough, when the door is opened for the ferret and he is allowed to be on the other side of the same door, he will immediately start digging on the opposite side wanting back where he began.

Keeping your ferret's front toenails trimmed short will help keep the digging damage to a minimum, but other than putting something dig-proof (such as a few ceramic tiles, a wide board, or other firm material) in front of the door, or wherever your ferret has chosen to dig, there is not much of a way to deter him from his appointed task.

Deafness

If you have established that some of the problem behaviors you've noted with your ferret are because he can't hear you, you'll have to come up with more creative ways to train him to know what you want. Remember, deafness in a ferret is not the life-altering experience it is for humans. In fact, most breeders believe that deafness is a far wider problem than is realized, simply because most people never realize their ferret is deaf at all. They compensate for their disability so easily that

I Can't Hear You

Don't panic if you learn that your ferret is deaf. It's not the big deal to them that it is to us humans. A ferret will compensate so readily to the disability that many pet owners will live with a ferret for his entire life without ever realizing he cannot hear. Ferrets quickly learn to adapt to reading your facial expressions, hand motions, and feeling for vibrations for signals as to what you expect from them.

If you have a deaf ferret, you will have to develop different training commands such as waving your fingers or turning a light on and off to get your ferret to come to you.

it's not uncommon for even the most dedicated ferret owner to never realize their ferret is lacking in any sensory perception.

One of the biggest complaints you may have from living with a deaf ferret is that he doesn't know when you're calling him. Some ferrets have been quickly trained to come to a laser light, a strobing flashlight, or even when their owner turns the room lights on and off. Just give the ferret a treat and positive attention (remember speaking to him won't help, and reinforcement will have to be in the form of hands-on attention)

Don't Worry

You may notice that your deaf ferret sleeps sounder than your other ferrets. At times he may almost seem to be in a coma. Don't panic. He will wake up when he's ready.

Practical Solutions to Outta Control Problems

Time to Give Up?

If you are absolutely certain that you have exhausted every avenue in dealing with your ferret and the bad behavior patterns continue to be something you cannot live with any longer, then it may be time to say goodbye. Do not just sell your ferret or give him away to another home that will be unable to deal with the problems either.

Find a ferret sanctuary or rescue network near you and discuss your options with the people who run it. Remember that even though your ferret may be driving you nuts, it is still a living breathing creature that deserves to have a suitable loving and permanent home. There truly is someone for everyone, and that goes for ferrets too.

when the ferret has responded correctly to whatever stimulus you choose.

You can teach your ferret to obey sign language if you are patient and consistent with the signs you use. Make sure you and everyone who works with your ferret always use the same sign for the same requested action, and make sure the ferret is always rewarded with a treat and positive attention when he reacts correctly. Some hand signals a ferret can quickly learn are to come to you when you lay your hand on the floor and waggle your fingers, or that a stomp of your foot means they've done something wrong. The vibration of this action is also useful as most deaf ferrets become very tuned to vibrations.

Preventing Problems Before They Start

The easiest way to deal with behavior problems is to prevent them before they become problems.

Never encourage bad behavior with your ferret. If you do not want him to do something, correct him and direct his attention elsewhere. Be consistent and patient when training your ferret.

Your ferrets are relying on you for love, safety, companionship, and the best possible care you can give them.

Practical Solutions to Outta Control Problems

* A ferret might bite when picked up because the owner doesn't know how to hold him. Be sure you know the proper way to pick up your ferret, but how to hold him so he feels secure.

* Never roughhouse with a ferret. You are in essence telling him that it is all right to wrestle and bite and nip his human. Instead, touch your ferret gently, rub his tummy, and stroke under his chin. Teach him that touch is a kind and gentle thing that he should learn to enjoy.

* Never allow any bad behavior once, much less encourage it, if it is a behavior that is not going to always be acceptable to you. Be consistent in your training and continue to love your ferret no matter how bad his behavior comes. You will soon find that your "outta control" ferret will quickly become the docile, gentle, sweet creature that nature intended him to be.

Your ferret will be with you for many years to come. Hopefully, by using this book, and with patience, time, and love you can help your ferret become not only a part of the household, but also a valued member of the family.

Resources

There are literally thousands of websites on the internet devoted to magazines and books about ferrets, ferret clubs, and ferret shelters and rescue networks, as well as a myriad of sites created to spotlight family pets, show champions, and breeding stock.

Doing a search on any search engine for 'ferret' will put you in contact with the thousands of other people who are interested in ferrets.

Magazines

Modern Ferret Magazine
PO Box 1007
Smithtown, NY 11787
Phone: (631) 981-3574
Fax: (631) 981-3710
Website: www.ModernFerretStore.com
Email: modferret@aol.com

Ferret Health Care and Shelters

Ferret News
www.ferretnews.org/clinic.html

Ferret Health Care
www.miamiferret.org/fhc

Ferret Central
(list of shelters, state by state)
www.ferretcentral.org/orgs.html#us

Everything Ferret
(list of shelters, state by state)
www.everythingferret.com/ferret_shelters.htm

Ferret Organizations and Associations

The American Ferret Association
PMB 255
626-C Admiral Dr.
Annapolis, MD 21401
Phone: 1-888-FERRET-1
Fax: (516) 908-5215
Website: www.ferret.org
Email: afa@ferret.org

Californians for Ferret Legalization
410 Mountain Home Road
Woodside, CA 94062
Phone: (650) 851-3750
Website: www.ferretnews.org
Email: ferretsnews@aol.com

Animal Protection Institute
1122 S Street
Sacramento, CA 95814 (or)
PO Box 22505
Sacramento, CA 95822
Phone: (916) 447-3085
Fax: (916) 447-3070
Website: api4animals.org
Email: info@api4animals.org

The National Humane Education Society
PO Box 340
Charles Town, WV 25414-0340
Phone: (304) 725-0506
Fax: (304) 725-1523
Website: www.nhes.org
Email: nhesinformation@nhes.org

The American Society for the Prevention of Cruelty to Animals (ASPCA)
424 East 92nd Street
New York, NY 10128
Phone: (212) 876-7700
Website: www.aspca.org

Ferret Wise Rescue & Rehabilitation Shelter
PO Box 561
Marlborough, NH 03455-561
Phone: (603) 876-4975
Website: www.ferretwise.org

Ferrets Anonymous
PO Box 6497
Torrance, CA 90504
Phone: (626) 358-6027
Website: www.ferretsanonymous.com
Email: FAmail@ferretsanonymous.com

S.T.A.R.
Pamela Troutman, Director
PO Box 1832
Springfield, VA 22151-0832
Phone: (703) 354-5073
Website: www.thepetproject.com/pam/starferrets.html
Email: STARFerret@aol.com

Best Friends Animal Sanctuary
Kanab, UT 84741-5000
Phone: (435) 644-2001
Website: www.bestfriends.org